A WALKER'S GUIDE TO NORTH DEVON

Rosemary Anne Lauder

Sixteen circular walks
with sketch maps

BADGER BOOKS

First published 1991

BADGER BOOKS
Dulverton, Somerset.

British Library Cataloguing in Publication Data
Lauder, Rosemary Anne
A Walker's Guide to North Devon
I. Title
914. 23504858

ISBN 0 946290 22 9

Cover Photograph: Sandra Yeo.
Printed in Great Britain by Maslands, Tiverton, Devon.

CONTENTS

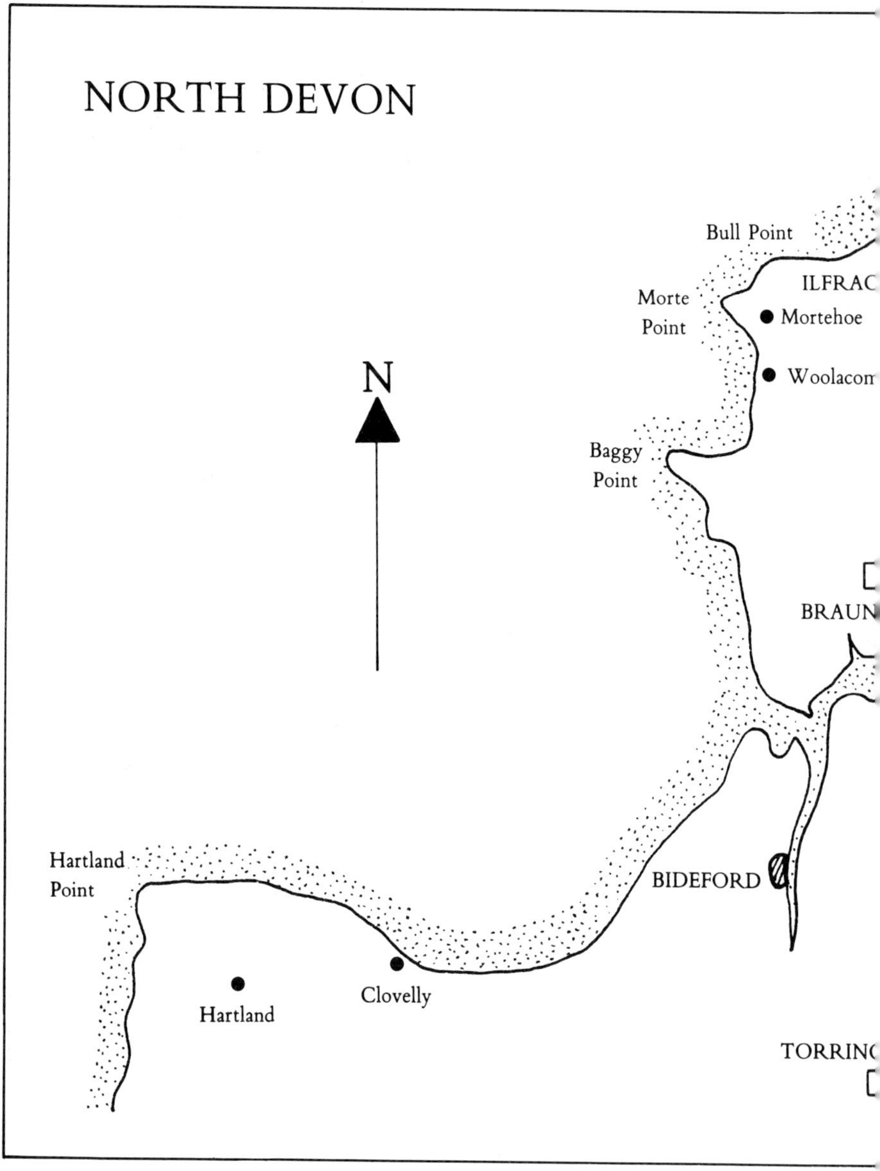

NORTH DEVON

N

Bull Point

ILFRAC

Morte
Point

Mortehoe

Woolacon

Baggy
Point

BRAUN

Hartland
Point

BIDEFORD

Clovelly

Hartland

TORRINC

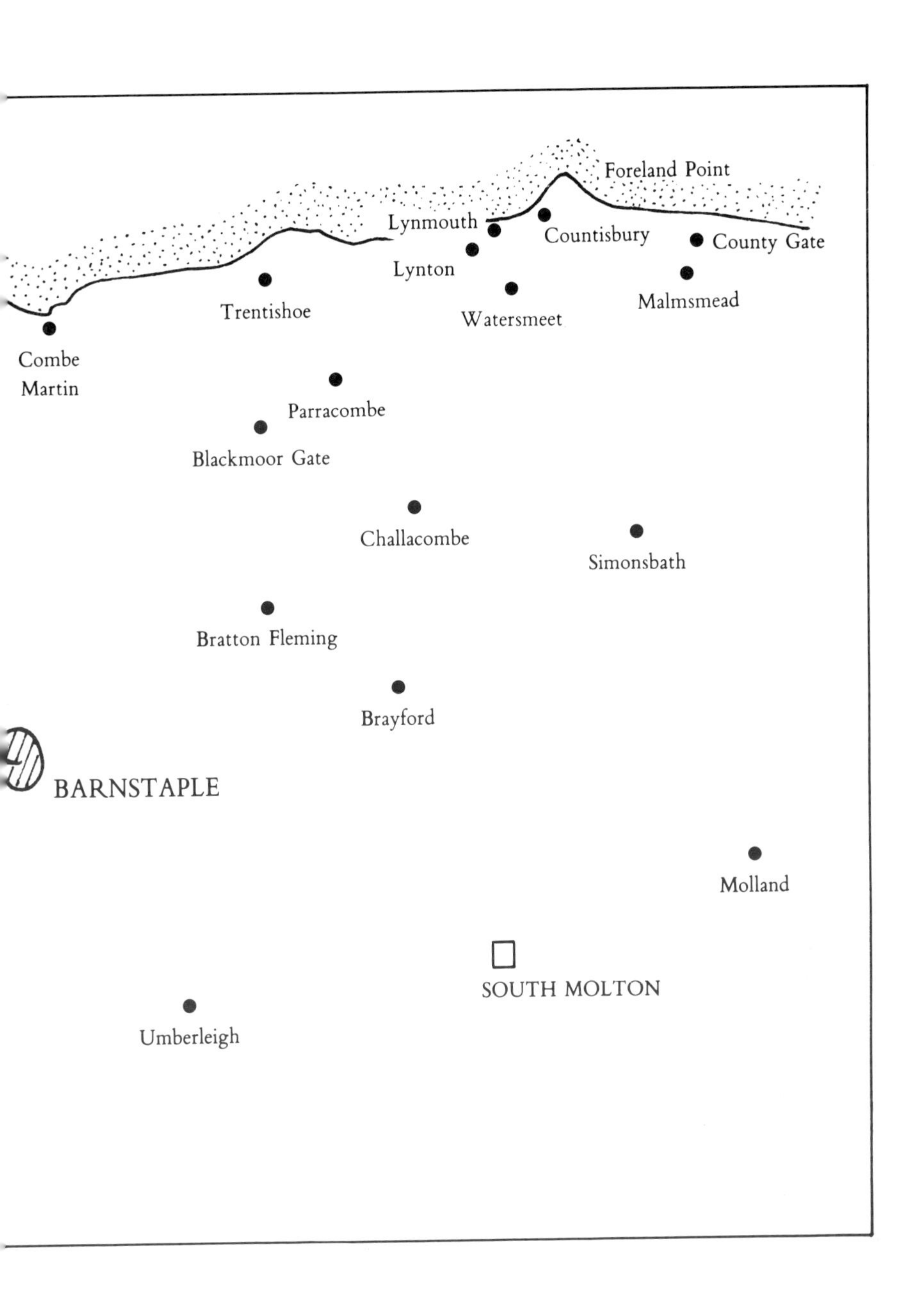
Foreland Point
Lynmouth
Countisbury
County Gate
Lynton
Trentishoe
Watersmeet
Malmsmead
Combe
Martin
Parracombe
Blackmoor Gate
Challacombe
Simonsbath
Bratton Fleming
Brayford
BARNSTAPLE
Molland
SOUTH MOLTON
Umberleigh

Introduction

What is there to attract a walker to North Devon? The county as a whole can offer Dartmoor with its moorland heights and miles of granite-strewn emptiness; it can offer a portion of Exmoor, with the recently created Two Moors Way linking the two. The long-distance footpath around the south west peninsula opened up the coasts in a most dramatic way to walkers, and brought large numbers of back-packers to previously unvisited headlands and coves. But long-distance walkers are a breed apart. I sometimes feel they wouldn't mind walking up the M1 as long as it was a recognised distance and a way-marked route, and they could boast about it in the pub afterwards.

North Devon can offer much that is fast disappearing elsewhere. In parts there is a remoteness rare in these overcrowded islands. It is still easy to escape the trappings of the twentieth century, easy to plan a route which avoids all habitations and places of refreshment. There are whole stretches of the coast where human homes are few and far between, and these are out of sight, sheltering a couple of miles inland.

Much of the hinterland of North Devon is farming country, but there are some good walks, and a long distance footpath to be known as the "Tarka Trail" is planned utilising two disused railway lines, largely following the journeys of Henry Williamson's famous otter.

Exmoor offers superb walking country, and that part which lies within Devon includes some of the best. It also includes some of the well known tourist haunts, such as Lynmouth, the Valley of the Rocks, and the Doone valley, but even here, out of season, there is fine scenery and a sense of isolation. Up on the moor are unspoilt hamlets and country inns, with folk living more or less as they have always lived – and hope to be allowed to continue to live.

About the Walks

In selecting the walks, there were several criteria. The most obvious is that they should be circular, few of us having the luxury of a car available to drop and pick up the walkers. The second is that they should combine good views, without which a walk is merely so much exercise, and the third is that roads should be avoided as far as possible. Many walks were tried and discarded, either because they could not be followed on the ground, looked they never so enticing on the map, or because the return route made use of busy roads or Devon lanes with no views and too much traffic.

Car parking was another important point. Many families include members who do not choose to walk, or are not capable of long distances, and pleasantly sited parking is an advantage all round. With most of the walks it is possible to begin at various points along the route, depending on where you are travelling from, and many of them can be cut short, or varied to suit your individual needs.

The scope of this book does not include the long-distance paths. These are not circular, and are usually undertaken by those who are more concerned about distance covered than enjoyment gained. They are also well documented already. The aim is that those of you who have limited time available, should not waste any of it on frustrating walks, but should enjoy the best North Devon has to offer.

No doubt I have missed out some people's favourite walk, but from a walker's view point I think these are the best. Many walks are obvious: Baggy Point, Braunton Burrows, Potters Hill above Woolacombe, for instance, are all worthwhile but need no help from me.

Only the marathon requires real walking fitness; and there should be no dangers on the routes because the walker is never far from habitation. Having said that, the weather can change quickly in Devon, and the wind can be surprisingly cold on the cliffs and moors, so that it pays to take adequate clothing, just in case.

I enjoyed every step – I hope you do!

* * *

The completion of the South West Way long distance coastal footpath has been hailed as a great achievement, yet in essence there is nothing new about it at all, and it has existed for well over one hundred years, as this extract proves. It is taken from "Devon Coasts, Moors and Rivers" written by W. Harding Thompson and published in 1932. The book was a form of survey published by the Council for the Protection of Rural England, and a chapter was devoted to "A Survey of the Coastal Tracks".

"In the course of this Survey the old coastal track has been followed from the Dorset boundary near Lyme Regis to Plymouth Sound; also from the Cornwall boundary at Marsland Mouth to the Somerset boundary at Glenthorne. In a few sections of the coast this track is a public footpath clearly marked, but, over the greatest part of its course, it runs through private estates where the public are allowed access to the track by the courtesy of the owners. Again, in some cases, where towns or villages have sea frontage, the construction of a public highway or promenade close to the cliffs has replaced the original coastguard route or rendered it unneccessary.

The Coastguard Service was empowered by Parliament to patrol any part of the coast in connection with their preventive work, and once a track had been formed by the continuous use of the patrols, it was natural that the local people and fishermen would make use of it for private reasons unconnected with the Coastguard Service. This custom and privilege has no doubt given rise to the claim, often stated, that there is a public right of way round the cliffs, even through private property. This claim of a public right has not been conclusively proved or substantiated in the courts; and although landowners have in many cases generously allowed the local inhabitants and tourists to make use of the old coastguard track through their estates, the owners have not thereby forfeited their right to close the track to any person except those engaged in coastguard work. On certain sections of the Devon coast the cliff track is beyond doubt a public right of way, but it is equally clear that in other sections the general public have no legal right of passage; they may not have been stopped by the landowner, but the latter would be well justified in closing the path if the privilege were abused by trespass, by wanton destruction of property, or by the scattering of litter.

It is hoped, nevertheless, that some means will be found, by agreement with the owners concerned, for the cliff track to be kept open for pedestrians, for in this way it would confer a very great benefit on all those who wish to enjoy the beauty of the Devon coast on foot and in close contact with the sea. In places where the cliff path crosses permanent pasture or rough grazing lands, it would appear unnecessary to confine the track between fences, except at points dangerous alike to man and beast; but, in cases where arable lands adjoin the cliffs, it may be advisable to fence off the track close to the edge of the cliff to avoid damage to crops by inconsiderate people. Since the reduction in personnel of the coastguard, and consquently a less frequent patrol service, the original track has fallen into disuse in several districts and has become overgrown with scrub or definitely blocked by farmers' fences. In spite of this, it is remarkable how much of the Devon coast can be visited on foot and how many delightful combes and headlands can be enjoyed which are inaccessible by road."

No doubt the author would be delighted to know that his hopes have been so completely realised, and that today every able-bodied walker is indeed at liberty to enjoy the beauty of the Devon coast and keep in close contact with the sea.

Badgworthy Water

Maps: OS Landranger 180.
Pathfinder SS 64/74.
Distance: 7 miles.

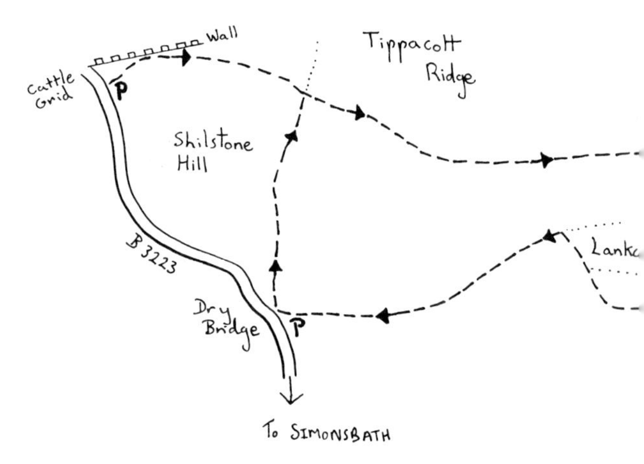

Walkers who dismiss the Doone country as being for motorists and coach parties will miss out on one of Exmoor's prettiest valleys. Forget the literary associations, and concentrate on the scenery.

The walk has been specifically planned to miss the worst of the crowds who congregate around Malmsmead and who may stroll a short distance up the valley; very few of them get as far as the supposed Doone valley (Hoccombe Combe) and none at all to the moor beyond. The higher stretches of Badgworthy Water (pronounced Badgery) are known only to serious walkers and riders. By starting the walk on the heights of the moor an interesting approach is gained, with far reaching views. But avoid the summer, the flies are as troublesome as the tourists and the open moorland can seem dreary with the views blurring into a haze.

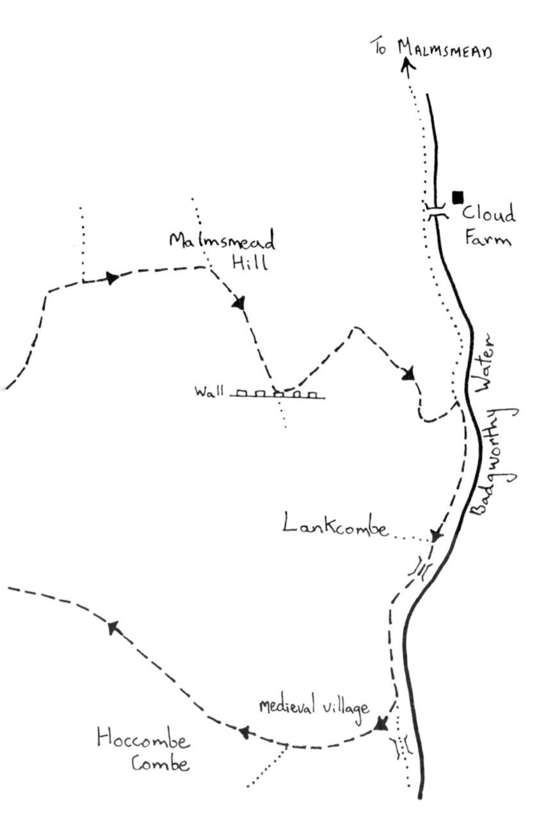

Start Point
Dry Bridge car park on the B3223 Simonsbath to Lynmouth road (or by the cattle grid further on).

Directions

Make for the summit of Shilstone Hill (1328 ft) and follow the red posts down to the broad track from the alternative start point.

Turn right and contour around the moor above the farmland, ignoring the tracks to the left to Brendon, and aiming for Malmsmead Hill (marked with a post).

The track from Malmsmead Hill comes down to meet the wall on your right. Do not go through the gate, but continue downhill, bearing to the left away from the wall.

From this narrow path there is a good view down over Badgworthy Water, with the white buildings of Cloud Farm prominent.

The path descends to meet the broad tourist track from Malmsmead.

A detour to Cloud Farm for refreshments can be made at this point. If so, the memorial stone to R.D. Blackmore will be passed. Grassy banks and rhododendrons make this area a pleasant place in which to linger.

Follow the track upstream, through the woods and out into the open.

Turn right away from Badgworthy up Hoccombe Combe (signposted). It is here that the remains of the medieval village can be seen to the left of the path – low grassy hummocks.

These are the remains of the village inhabited by the Doones, according to legend. The famous romance of Lorna Doone is a curious phenomena. In itself, it is a book well worth reading – but that a somewhat long, and in places, prosy novel should have inspired such a tourist boom and should continue to draw visitors by the coachload, is remarkable. Blackmore was surprised by the novel's success and would be even more surprised to know that it continues up to the present day. Had he known, he might have ended the controversy as to whether the Doones really existed, or whether he invented the whole story, or adapted a legend.

Hoccombe Combe can be followed to its head on Brendon Common, but a tedious tramp across the heather or a stretch of road walking is required to regain the car park.

Take the footpath to the right at the junction, away from Hoccombe Combe. It follows a minor valley up on to the moor. Go through the gate in the stone wall and keep straight ahead to join the path from Dry Bridge to Malmsmead.

Turn left back to the car park.

Glenthorne

Glenthorne for many is a romantic spot. The steep combe is reliably linked with smuggling. It is strangely secretive, the lower slopes being invisible from the road and most of the rest of the coast. Although the coastal footpath was routed through the combe, there was no access from the estate itself, which remained strictly private until recently when a management agreement was reached with the National Park.

Glenthorne was the creation of one man, the Reverend Walter Halliday. He was left a legacy in the 1820's and left his native Isle of Wight to search for a suitable property to become his country estate. His choice fell on Glenthorne and over a peiod of years he acquired the whole of the valley and much surrounding land, extending to 6,000 acres and including part of the Watersmeet estate.

The Halliday's continued at Glenthorne until 1983 when the National Trust acquired the cliffs to the west, but not the house itself which was sold privately.

This whole area is rapidly becoming a popular walkers' and naturalists' paradise. It has the added advantage of being sheltered from the cold north and easterly winds, even from the westerlies.

From the car park there are views over the Valley to Malmsmead Hill.

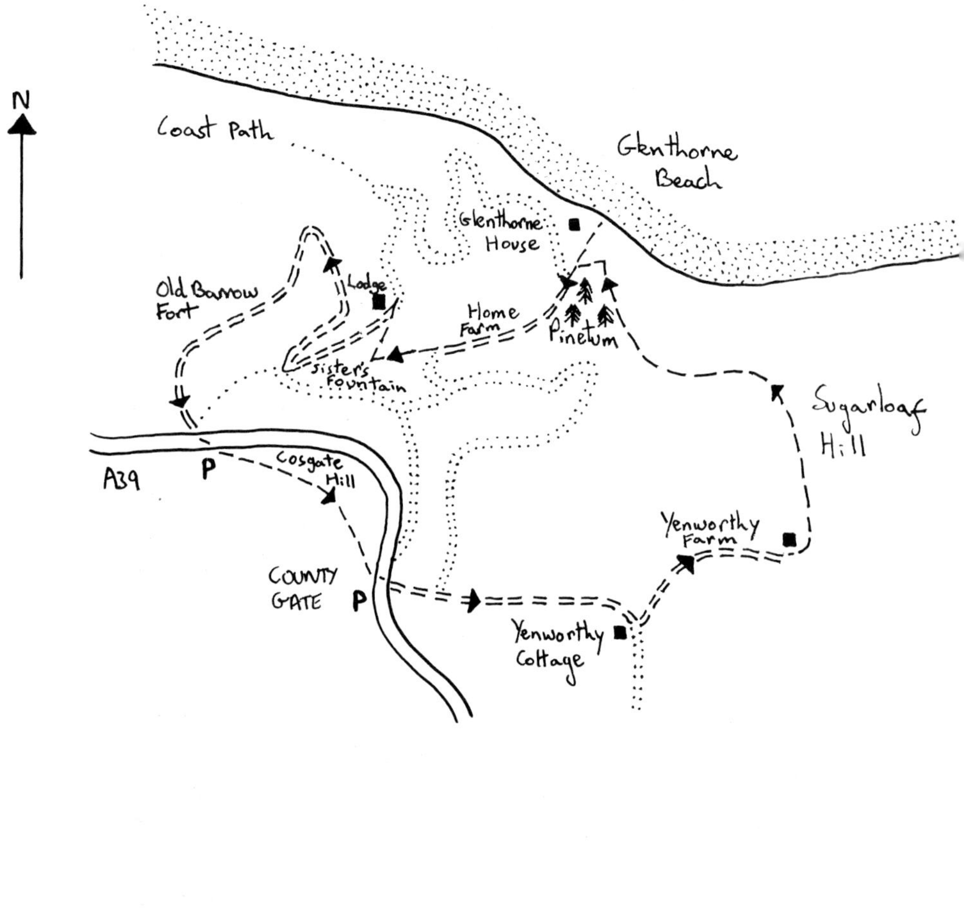

N

Coast Path

Glenthorne Beach

Glenthorne House

Old Barrow Fort

Lodge

Home Farm

Pinetum

Sister's Fountain

Sugarloaf Hill

A39

P

Cosgate Hill

Yenworthy Farm

COUNTY GATE

P

Yenworthy Cottage

Directions

Cross the main road and follow the bridlepath to Culbone which goes gently downhill. At Yenworthy Cottage turn off the main track, which turns right uphill, and continue on the path, marked red, to Yenworthy Farm.

This ancient and attractive farm dates from the mid 1600's, although altered and "gothicised" in the 1850's. It has a claim to fame in that it appears in "Lorna Doone", its occupants being one of the few inhabitants of the area who were prepared to stand up to the brigands. The long gun with which the Widow Fisher is supposed to have taught the Doone's a lesson is still kept at the farmhouse, once part of the Glenthorne Estate.

Bear left behind the farmhouse, and take the wooden gate (left hand one of the two). There are no markings, but cross the fields towards Sugarloaf Hill, keeping close to the hedge.

Sugarloaf Hill (named by the Rev. Halliday) overlooks the whole valley and from the second seat are the best views of Glenthorne House. The view also includes Porlock Bay to the east, and the whole glorious cliff panorama of oak woods, rhododendrons, and conifers.

Follow the stone wall downhill and take the path, signposted to Culbone and Glenthorne Beach, to the right. This follows the stream, and can be continued right down to the beach. The two paths through the woods meet lower down.

The pinetum was planted by the Rev. Halliday from 1840 onwards, and there are some fine species, now fully mature. They include cypress, the maidenhair tree, cedar, hemlock, Wellingtonia, pine and spruce. The National Park leaflet, "Walks from County Gate", gives a detailed map. The detour to the beach is not necessary, but the walker might feel he should walk the whole length of the glen, from top to bottom, a drop of some one thousand feet. Boulders and pebbles make swimming something of an endurance test, and in the days when boats carrying coal and building materials discharged on the beach, it had first to be cleared of the larger boulders. It must have been very hard work. It is also supposed to have been a favourite with the smuggler's – and it isn't hard to see why.

Continue on the path signposted County Gate via Sister's Fountain, and turn uphill on the drive from Glenthorne House. This leads to Home Farm.

Home Farm is now in a state of neglect, and very little farming has been carried on for a century. The extensive farm buildings included piggeries and cowsheds, although some of these were damaged in the torrential rains of 1952. The farm was built around the same time as Glenthorne house and the valley contains evidence of former cultivation and of irrigation ponds.

Turn right down the narrow path opposite the signpost to County Gate and Sister's Fountain, which needs to be watched for. The path dips to cross the stream where a sign warns that adders are breeding – was this an early version of the bull-in-field ploy? – and there is the rhythmic sound of a hydraulic ram.

Sister's Fountain was named after the nieces of the Rev. Halliday, and is marked by a large cross, more reminiscent of a memorial than of a favourite spot.

Turn left uphill where the path meets the main drive, just above the entrance gates. Notice the boar's heads surmounting the pillars.

The drive is a fine piece of road building, and makes for easy walking as the gradients are well planned. From the road down to the house the drive drops some 950 feet over a distance of three miles, with several hairpin bends.

Where the main track from Coscombe joins, a signpost points straight up the valley to County Gate. This is steep and can be wet, and is best ignored. Keep to the drive, from which the glen can be appreciated, and which is altogether more leisurely. From the bend, in particular, are fine views.

A path to the right leads to the Old Barrow, a Roman hill fort, now surrounded by forestry.

Follow the main drive back up to the main road, and cross over. A path leads around Cosgate Hill back to County Gate car park, avoiding walking back along the road, and giving totally different views over the East Lyn valley.

County Gate to Malmsmead

Distance: 3 miles, one steep climb.

Start Point: **County Gate** car park, free.
Malmsmead.

Maps: OS Landranger 180
Pathfinder SS 64/74
"Walks from County Gate" Exmoor National Park leaflet.

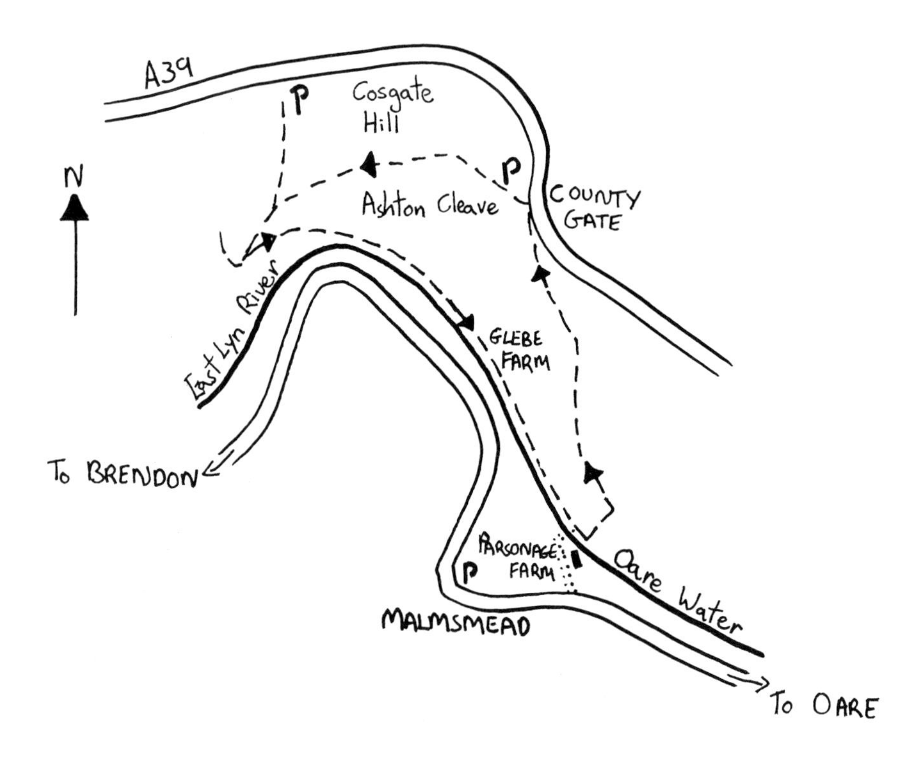

County Gate, the boundary between Devon and Somerset, is marked by a small cottage that served as a toll house when the gate across the road was still in existence. It was said of the gatekeeper that he slept with his head in one county and his feet in another! The cottage is now run by the Exmoor National Park authority as a visitor centre and shop. It also serves light snacks, drinks, ices etc.

The large car park behind the centre overlooks the valley of the East Lyn. Beyond are the heights of Exmoor – Brendon Common, Malmsmead Hill, Dunkery on a clear day, and to the left, the deep cleft of Badgworthy Water, part of the Doone country. It is another of those useful places where non-walking members can be left with plenty to occupy them.

Apart from the views, which are delineated on a "viewfinder board", there is a memorial to the writer, J.B.H. Peel. He was a well known writer on the countryside, and country matters, contributing regularly to the Daily Telegraph for many years. He retired to Parracombe and died in 1984.

Directions

Leave the car park by the footpath to the right, signposted to Malmsmead (1½ miles). This travels away from your destination, giving views downstream towards Brendon and Rockford. To the left is a steep scree slope. Where the path from Cosgate Hill (an alternative car park) comes down from the right, turn left back on yourself, and follow the path down to the riverbank.

The East Lyn here is broad, with rippling shallows and several deep and secretive pools among the overhanging branches. On hot days the temptation may prove too great, and you will not be the first to cool off in the clean, moorland water, stretching out to dry on the rocks afterwards.

Continue up the riverbank. Formerly the path circumnavigated the small field, but permission has been negotiated for it to keep to the riverbank, where it passes in front of Glebe farmhouse, through a gate and into a field.

At the footbridge, cross to the other bank and follow the track past Parsonage farm to the road.

Turn right down to Malmsmead.

It is not necessary to visit Malmsmead; if this is the case, do not cross the river.

Malmsmead was once an insignificant collection of cottages by the ford, with a pretty bridge to add to its picturesqueness. Then along came Mr Blackmore with his tales of Lorna Doone, and now Malmsmead is a busy little place, with coaches and streams of visitors. Most of them, however, never stray from the car park, gift shop and restaurant.

A detour to Cloud Farm is worth making for two reasons; the first is the excellent home-made food, drinks, ices etc., available in pleasant surroundings; the second is that it enables the lower reaches of Badgworthy Water to be explored. Cloud Farm is well signposted from the road before Malmsmead is reached.

The Exmoor Natural History Centre is also passed on the way to Malmsmead. This contains a small but interesting display, well worth a visit if you are passing on a Wednesday or Thursday afternoon between May and September.

Return to the bridge and recross the water.

Turn right for a short distance, then left between hedgebanks topped with trees, into a field. Aim for the gate at the base of the hillside, signposted Malmsmead ¾ mile, and begin the ascent. Once the wire fence is reached you are almost there. The path begins to level out and a gate takes you out onto the road by the car park.

Countisbury to Rockford

From the heights of Countisbury, to the depths of Rockford – this is a dramatic walk. Within a very short distance from Lynmouth the cliffs soar to over one thousand feet, the highest cliffs in Devon, and the most northerly. There is a beach far, far below at Sillery Sands but, strange to say, it is not well frequented! No, this part of the county is walkers' country. Nothing much to attract the beach brigade, and a corresponding shortage of ice cream vans and cafes, which is all to the good. (Most of the walk is over National Trust land and is therefore well signposted, with reasonably good paths. The Trust has been acquiring land in this area since 1934 and now has the major part of the cliffs and Lyn Cleave in safe-keeping.)

Rockford is a small hamlet buried deep at the bottom of the valley of the East Lyn, tree surrounded and built on the very edge of the water, uncomfortably close at times.

It makes a good goal as there is an inn, and a restaurant, open in the season only. There is very little parking space, so it is not feasible to do this walk in reverse, although many would prefer to have the steep climb before lunch, and finish with the descent. Sorry, you can't have everything.

The car park at the top of Countisbury Hill is a very airy spot. Look for the parking sign on the bend beyond the inn. This is the Barna Barrow car park, 1,057 feet above sea level.

Maps: OS Landranger 180.
Pathfinder SS 64/74.
NT Leaflets "Countisbury and Glenthorne Cliffs" and "Watersmeet".

Distance: 4½ miles.

Start Point: Barna Barrow car park.

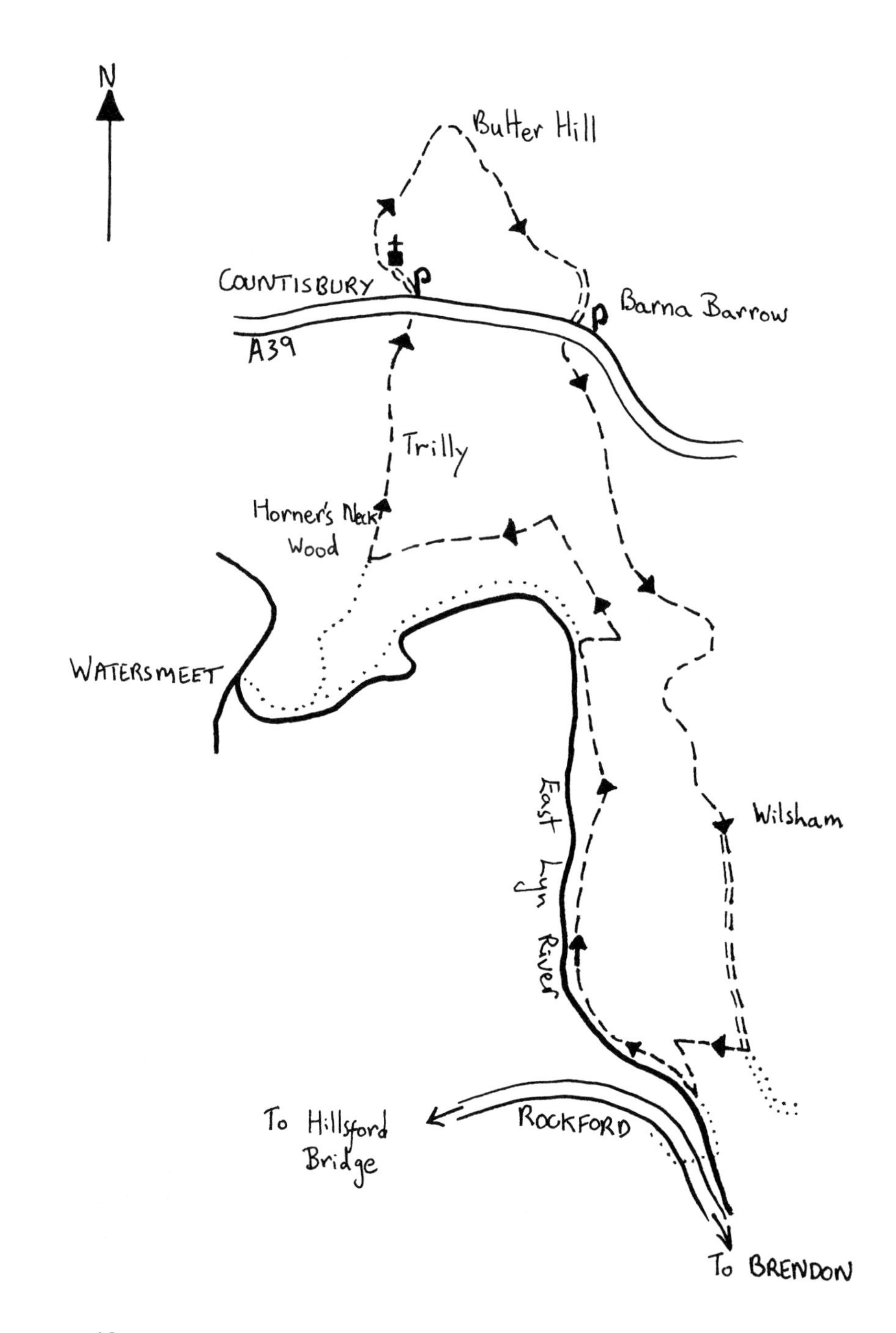
N
Butter Hill
COUNTISBURY
Barna Barrow
A39
Trilly
Horner's Neck Wood
WATERSMEET
East Lyn River
Wilsham
To Hillsford Bridge
ROCKFORD
To BRENDON

Directions

Cross the main road and go through the gate signposted to Rockford. Follow the yellow marks as the path winds around the valley to the hamlet of Wilsham. There is one damp place when crossing a stream, which could be awkward after heavy rain. This path is not as well frequented as many of the others in the area, otherwise stepping stones or a small bridge would have been provided. Follow the track uphill, not the narrow path to the right.

There is nothing much at Wilsham except some attractive cottages, farm buildings and a duck pond.

The path passes above the cottages and crosses the lane. Follow the farm track until a yellow marked gate on the right.

Turn right through the gate and double back down the hill, and again turn sharply as you enter Wilsham Wood. This leads down to the river bank.

The path to Rockford is straightforward, and the river is crossed via a footbridge.

There is no need to proceed as far as Rockford unless in need of sustenance. The village is situated on an ancient crossing the the East Lyn, and the ford is still obvious, though little used now as there is a footbridge.

To return, retrace your steps and continue along the riverbank, downstream, until a signpost to Countisbury points up through the woods.

The path follows a stream as far as a padlocked gate, here turn to the left.

The path winds around the valley through the woods, emerging at Horner's Neck.

An isthmus of high land juts out into the cleave high above Watersmeet, and formed by the confluence of the two streams. Its top is bare of trees, and were it not for the dense foliage of the oaks that clothe the sides, would be a viewpoint of some excellence. As it is, only tantalising glimpses can be gained through the branches, but it is worth a stroll to the end just the same.

Take the footpath that crosses the fields signposted to Countisbury. This emerges on the main road; turn left downhill.

Countisbury is a small cluster of church, inn and cottages, one of which was once a school. The round chimneys of the cottages are a feature. The inn for most of its long life has been known as the Blue Ball, but new owners decided on a new name, though everyone for miles around knows where you mean when you mention the Blue Ball.

The church has been the subject of much restoration and rebuilding and the most noteworthy object is the Chancel screen with a late 17th century pediment added.

Visit the church and follow the path through the churchyard and out onto the cliffs.

The quickest route back to the car is to follow the wall. This detour avoids walking along the busy main road.

Strike out across the open headland to Butter Hill, which at 993 feet is a commanding viewpoint.

This former signal station has been adapted to modern needs, but also provides some shelter to walkers caught in a sudden squall in this very exposed place. The views on a clear day extend across the Channel to Wales, power stations and all, and inland across Brendon Common, and over Lynmouth and Lynton. It is well worth the very small extra effort required and provides a complete contrast with the sylvan nature of the rest of the walk.

Lyn Cleave and Countisbury

This is a fine walk amongst the beauties of the East Lyn river and the steeply wooded cleave. The narrow ridge of land that separates the sea from Lyn Cleave is Countisbury Hill, notorious with an earlier generation of motorists for its steepness, and equally feared by coach drivers and their passengers (the horsedrawn variety, not today's mobile glasshouses). From Countisbury, the land falls away steeply to Sillery Sands over 800 feet below, giving fine sea views, whilst inland the eye takes in Brendon and Malmsmead Commons, and even Dunkery itself on a clear day.

The walk can be treated as a short expedition, or can be extended to last most of the day, with stops at Watersmeet and Rockford and a final halt at Countisbury.

It is possible to begin the walk from either of the first named places, but parking is limited and expensive at Watersmeet, and virtually non-existent at Rockford, except by courtesy of the landlord if you are a good customer.

Directions

From the public car park at the top of Countisbury Hill, opposite the Sandpiper Inn, walk downhill on the road to the first gateway on the left, which is at the head of Chisel Combe.

Bear left around the manmade pond on the path named "Winston's path" to Watersmeet.

Winston is the name of the National Trust local warden who carried out much of the construction work on this path.

Distance: 4-5 miles.
Start Point: Countisbury car park, free.
Maps: OS Landranger 180.
Pathfinder SS 64/74.

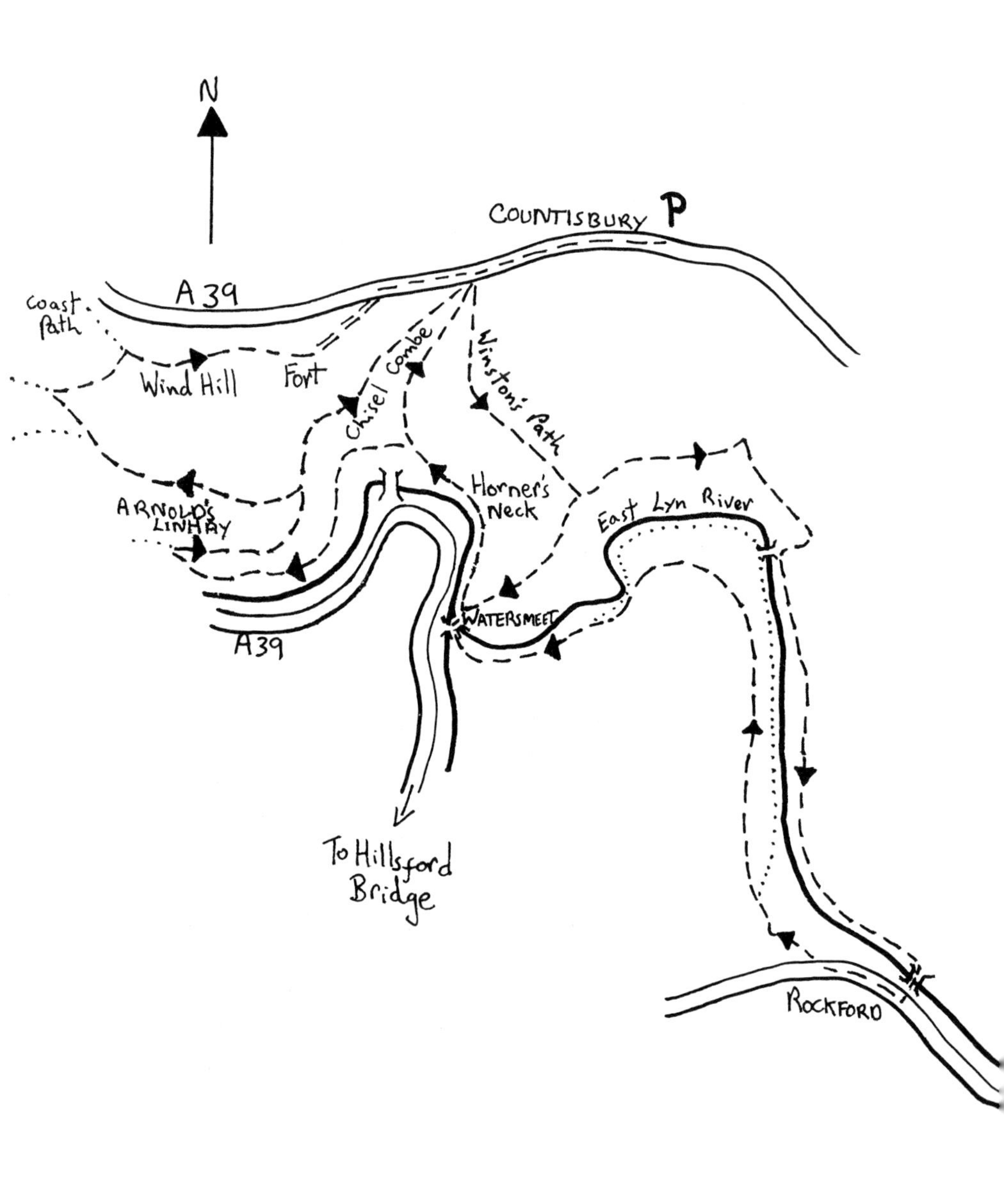

After a gentle incline, the path levels out and contours around the cleave above the tree line, to arrive at Horner's Neck.

From the grassy ridge what should be spectacular views in all directions are masked by the oak trees; perhaps Winston could be prevailed upon to create just one or two glimpses?

From Horner's Neck there are two choices; the longer walk continues on the high level path to **Rockford**. It is well signposted and eventually descends to the river bank, which follow until the footbridge a short distance beyond Rockford. Cross and walk back to the village.

The return journey to Watersmeet can be made along either bank of the East Lyn, the bridlepath on the Rockford side beginning a short way beyond the houses, just as the road begins to climb. This is the easiest path.

For **Watersmeet,** descend from Horner's Neck down a steep path.

The National Trust shop offers refreshments (see the Watersmeet walk for details). The waterfalls and restored limekiln are worth a visit, and it is a good spot for sitting and watching the water and bird life.

Turn right downstream without crossing the river, and continue on this bank until the footpath to the right (to Countisbury) is reached. This returns to Chisel Combe.

Extend the walk by continuing along the path, taking the next higher path and then sharp right on Arnold's Linhay path, to join the high level path from Countisbury.

Turn left. The path contours above the trees giving fine views across the cleave and down towards Lynmouth.

After some distance the path divides, that to Lynmouth turning downhill (Sparrow's Path) and that to Wind Hill bearing right and uphill, signposted coastal path.

Follow the path out onto the open hillside and detour to the left along the ridge for a bird's eye view over

Lynmouth, before retracing your steps, and following the path which drops on the seaward side to meet the coastal path proper coming up from Lynmouth.

Turn right uphill again to the summit of Wind Hill, 854ft.

This ancient earthwork fortress was the scene of a battle in 878 between the local inhabitants, under their chief, Cynuit, and Hubba the Dane, who lost! It is considered that the name Countisbury derives from Cynuit's fort, or burg. At all events, it is a splendid viewpoint and there is a display board recounting the story.

The track leads back down to the road and thence to the car park.

If Butter Hill has not yet been visited (see Countisbury to Rockford Walk), now is a good opportunity; walk through the churchyard and out onto the headland. Butter Hill is 993 feet above the sea, and worth the extra effort.

Watersmeet

Maps: OS Landranger 180.
Pathfinder SS 64/74.
NT Leaflet "Watersmeet".
NP Leaflets "Watersmeet" and "Countisbury & Glenthorne".
Distance: At least 5 miles.

The woodlands of the steep-sided East Lyn gorge, and the sparkling, tumbling waters of the river make an expedition along its course a must for all visitors to the area. Many will stroll for less than a mile along the river bank from Lynmouth or Watersmeet, or from Hillsford Bridge on the Hoaroak Water, but even in such a short distance they will have enjoyed a taste of beauty nonetheless.

For the more energetic, the permutations are endless and can include some steep climbs, for the sides of the Lyn Gorge rise over 900 feet, giving amazing views. Here is mountain scenery in miniature, the steep falls and sudden views belying the relatively small scale of the landscape.

The Watersmeet estate passed into the hands of the National Trust in 1934–36, with significant additions over the years to include the coastal lands and all of the river valley between Hillsford Bridge and Lynmouth, with the exception of a few private houses. An abundance of footpaths criss-crosses the woodlands,and the three bridges between Lynmouth and Watersmeet allow many permutations, but it must be stressed there is no continuous footpath on the south bank (right side as you go upstream), and the road is close by with a constant stream of traffic in the summer months.

It should also be stressed that the footpath along the north bank, is NOT a gentle, level stroll, although it may look like it on the map.

A walk around the valley, or cleave, of the Lyn is one of the best for contrasts. The views take in the grandeur of the high level panoramas, with the back drop of the untamed moorland. The steep cleave frames Lynmouth with the sea beyond, and the valley bottom far below, clothed in dense woodland. The trees are largely oak and beech, but there are some less usual species, mainly whitebeam (sorbus), and a wealth of smaller plants including broom, and whortleberries. Down by the river, the constant movement of the water over its rocky bed is endlessly fascinating, and the varied bird life makes interesting watching. After heavy rain, the water level rises dramatically and the Lyn becomes a muddy, rushing torrent.

Start Point: Most people will begin from Lynmouth, but an alternative is **Hillsford Bridge** where the NT provide a large, grassy car park amongst some fine trees. **Countisbury** is another possibility, using the public car park opposite the inn.

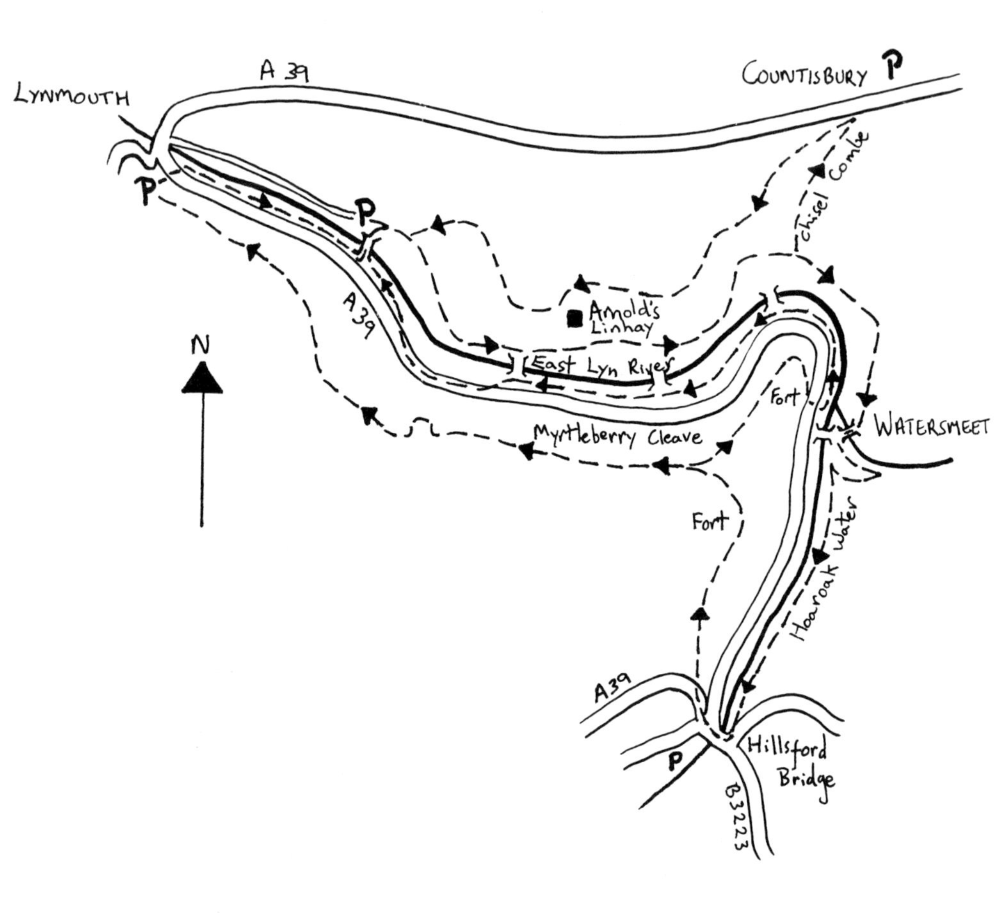

Directions

From **Lynmouth**, park either in the large car park off the Simonsbath road, or follow the narrow lane on the opposite bank, (turn right immediately after crossing the bridge), and leave the car at the end where there is a small, shady parking area (free). Follow the river upstream on either bank.

The footpath on the righthand bank passes the site of ten cottages at Middleham, of which only the gardens now remain; they were washed away in the 1952 flood. The Lynmouth Mineral Water Factory suffered the same fate, and its site is recorded by a bottle in the wall, and presumably the fountain issuing from the bank is the spring – it tastes jolly good!

Cross to the left bank at the first bridge and take the path signposted to Arnold's Linhay and Countisbury.

According to local tradition, the linhay (small barn) was where 'Arnold' kept his donkeys and mules used in transporting goods along the wellworn path from Lynmouth, in daily use before the building of the coast road up Countisbury Hill.

Look for the wild broom with its small yellow flowers, and in the autumn for the abundance of "whorts" – whortleberries – providing a delicious free feast of small purple fruits if you are lucky enough to get to them first.

Follow the signposts, which now say Watersmeet, and after contouring along at mid-valley height, the path descends to the river bank.

Enjoy the views over the cleave, and the delightful property of Myrtleberry with its lovely gardens.

The graceful arched bridge was built across the East Lyn to replace that swept away in 1952. It serves the National Trust shop and restaurant at Watersmeet, but is not for motorists, only pedestrians.

Continue along the left bank to Watersmeet, where the East Lyn is joined by the Hoaroak Water, both of which are crossed by wooden bridges. Most of the streams on Exmoor are known as "waters" – neither streams nor rivers.

The quaint, rustic building at Watersmeet was built around 1830 and was a fishing lodge belonging to the Glenthorne Estate (at County Gate). It is a pretty spot and makes an excellent halt offering refreshments and a well-stocked shop.

For a **shorter return**, retrace your steps on the north bank (righthand going downstream) and follow the path to the right, signposted Countisbury. This ascends Chisel Combe.

Turn left just before reaching the main road (unless a visit to Countisbury is planned) and keep to the high level path until "Sparrows Walk" is reached. This is a steep descent to the river, and the path back to Lynmouth.

For a short deviation with some fine views over Lynmouth, follow the "coast path" sign and follow the deviation to the left which will bring you to Beacon Tor, with a bird's eye view.

For a much **longer walk**, cross the first bridge at Watersmeet and amble gently up the East Lyn passing the mine adit, to look at the reconstructed limekiln. This is a detour, and can be omitted.

The woodlands were once busy with charcoal burners, and packhorses bringing lime to be burnt, though it seems a strangely remote spot in which to site the kiln. Together with the mining activities it must have been quite active and populous.

Turn back, keeping to the higher path, and climb gently up alongside the Hoaroak Water to Hillsford Bridge.

Turn up on the A39 main road and at the first hairpin bend, leave the road and go through the gate, marked M/W for the Two Moors Way, and with a NT sign "Watersmeet Estate"

Ignore the path that turns down to the right, signposted to Watersmeet. This is the most direct route, but it misses all the good views.

At the junction a little further along, from where the valley of the cleave opens up with a view down to Lynmouth, there is a choice.

Either turn down to the right, to Watersmeet. To avoid erosion steps have been constructed which are awkwardly spaced and tedious. A bypass path to the right is proving popular, rejoining at the bottom.

The path passes Myrtleberry camp, an iron age fortification which has recently been cleared of scrub and provides a good resting spot with fine views, especailly across the cleave to Horner's Neck Wood.

The path descends steeply to the main road. **WARNING:** ensure children and dogs are under control as it is a sudden emergence.

Cross quickly and take the footpath that leaves the layby opposite from the left hand corner.

Follow the river bank downstream on whichever bank is preferred. The left bank includes a steep climb around Myrtleberry, and one section on the main road.

OR

For those who like to stay above the tree line, and have some spare energy, the high level path to Lynmouth is rewarding, particularly on a fine day.

Continue on from the junction. The path is never in doubt and ends up descending between the cottages close to the car park. But is is not a level, downhill-all-the-way path, having one sharp down and up section around a small tributary valley.

The Walker's Marathon

This is for the dedicated walker, for the hardy soul who likes to be out all day. Most of the walks contained in this book can be comfortably completed in a morning or an afternoon, although it is quite possible to spin them out to last much longer. Only by starting early, or finishing late, could the marathon fit into half a day. And there would be no sense in rushing it, for throughout its length it is great walking, a delight to the feet and to the eye.

Although it is the longest walk, it has the shortest directions. This is because the route is easy to follow, and much of it forms part of one of the other walks, so that these can be referred to if in doubt. Walkers experienced in following maps, and that should be you, will not need detailed instructions. In fact, there are many variations that can be carried out, once you have realised the general direction of the route.

The idea was to devise a circular walk that would include as many elements of Exmoor as possible, and that would avoid roads. This has been achieved, with a short length of minor road at Rockford being the only tarmacced stretch. Some of the busier places of the moor could not be avoided – and they do have the advantage of providing refreshment!

There are four possible start points (five if you include Watersmeet), and the walk is worthwhile in either direction, but the clockwise direction (looking at the map) is preferred as the views are better.

The circle follows the coast from Butter Hill to Glenthorne (or to Old Barrow), then descends to the valley of the East Lyn at Malmsmead. Badgworthy Water can be intolerably crowded, but most coach party people only stroll a very short distance, and will soon be outdistanced by the serious walker. The heights of Malmsmead common will almost certainly be empty of other human beings, and the descent to Rockford is over quiet farmland.

The wooded valley of the East Lyn to Watersmeet is always a delight and from here the climb back up can be made either via Wind Hill or direct to Countisbury or Barna Barrow.

Refreshments are available at County Gate, Malmsmead, Cloud Farm (Doone valley), Rockford, Watersmeet and Countisbury.

If you have saved this for the last day of your holiday, then you will return home with an abiding memory of all that is best on Exmoor.

Start Points
Barna Barrow car park (above Countisbury).
County Gate or **Cosgate Hill**
Dry Bridges or the park by the cattle grid on the **B3223** Simonsbath Lynmouth road.
Malmsmead Hill or Tippacott Ridge – open moorland on the minor road from Brendon to Malmsmead.
Watersmeet if you are early and don't mind paying.

Directions
These are given from **Barna Barrow**, and are divided into sections for easy reference.

Follow the track through the National Trust gates and out onto the open headland. Bear round to the right on a well defined path to **Kipscombe**. Cross the road to the lighthouse and take a good look at the fields beyond Kipscombe farmhouse. The path crosses the fields to the right of the hedge boundary, and the position of the gates should be noted as they cannot be seen when actually in the relevant fields.

The path leaves Kipscombe via the lorry parking area, marked by a small yellow arrow on the gate – or aim for the tall beech trees. The gates ahead are all yellow-marked.

Maps: OS Landranger 180.
Pathfinder SS 64/74.
Distance: 16 miles.

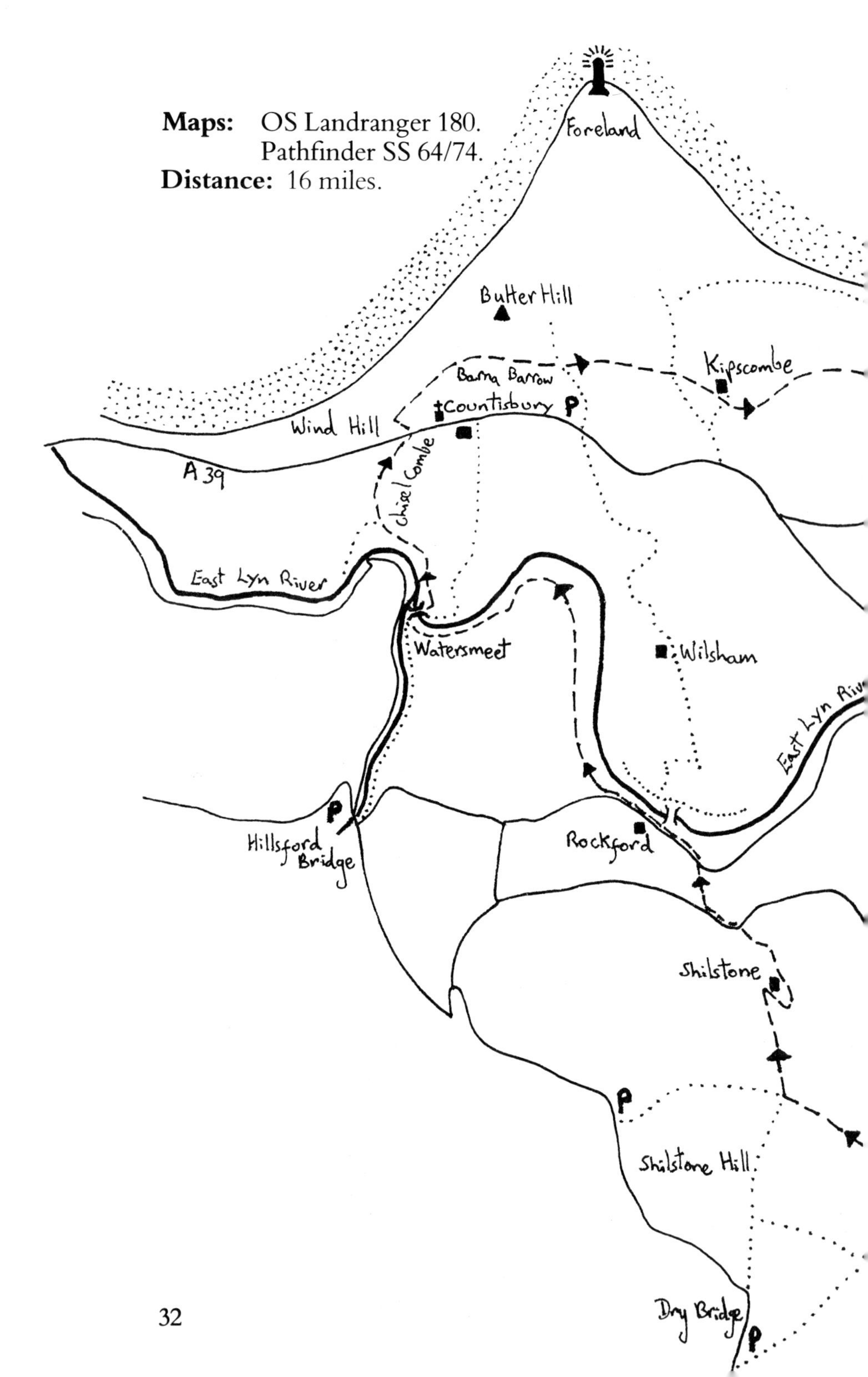

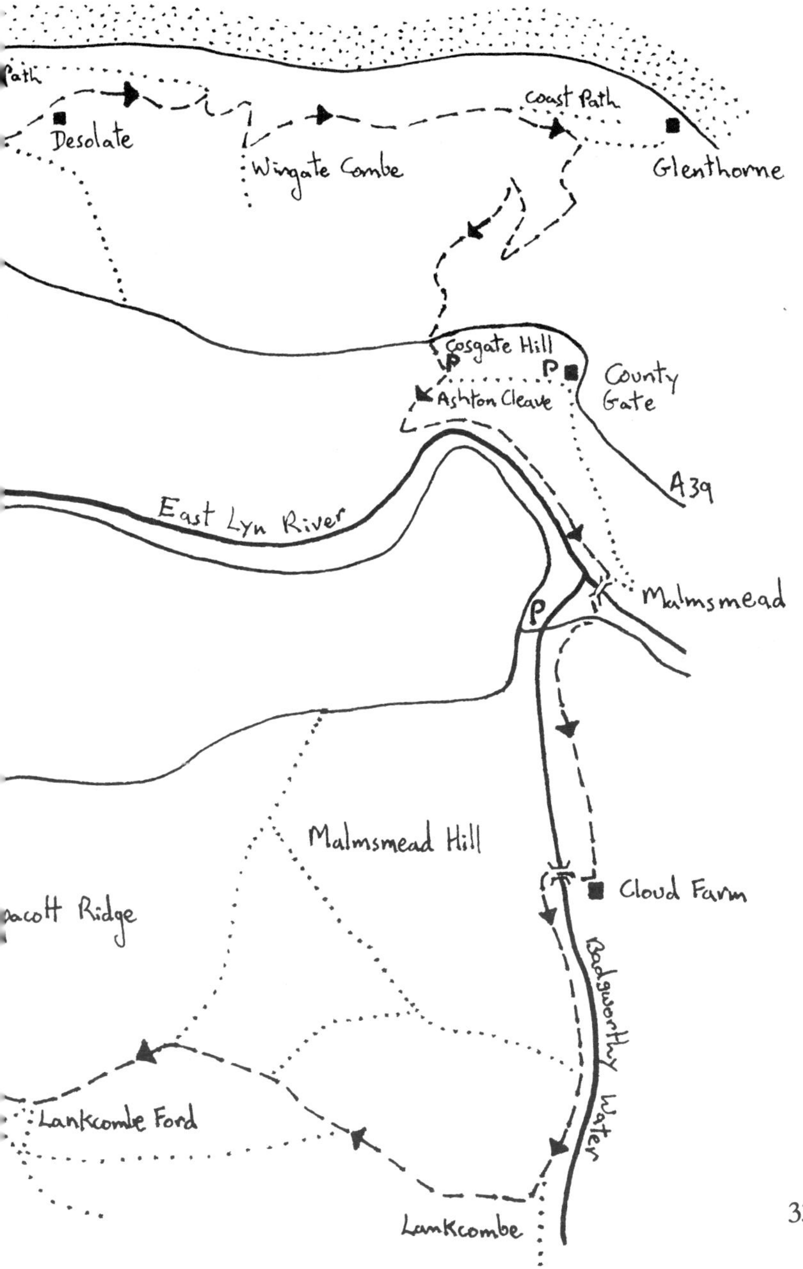

Path
Desolate
Wingate Combe
Coast Path
Glenthorne
Cosgate Hill
P
P
County Gate
Ashton Cleave
A39
East Lyn River
Malmsmead
P
Malmsmead Hill
Cloud Farm
acott Ridge
Badgworthy Water
Lankcombe Ford
Lankcombe

On reaching a track, turn left through the gate in the stone wall signposted 'Desolate and the coast path'. This junction could be missed, so watch for the track which leads down to the farmhouse. The path continues beyond, descending to join the coast path. The views from this section are good, especially back towards the Foreland.

The coast path winds on, round Wingate Combe where a path leads up to the main road. From here onwards is rhododendron country. Whilst the riot of pink flowers in June is a magnificent sight, the rapid growth of this alien shrub quickly obliterates everything else, and were it not ruthlessly hacked back, would make walking an impossibility. The Glenthorne estate is entered with evidence of stonework, seats etc.

Turn right uphill signposted to Culbone and County Gate.

The path climbs steadily to meet the Glenthorne Estate drive; turn right and gain the main road, which cross straight over on to **Cosgate Hill**.

County Gate is reached by turning to the left, otherwise continue straight down and join the path from County Gate to Malmsmead which descends via the steep scree slope of Ashton Cleave to Oare Water

Descend to the water, and if it is spring, watch for the resident family of ducklings splashing amongst the deep, cool pools.

The path follows the river bank to the footbridge to **Malmsmead**.

Here the path from **County Gate** joins.

Cross the river and walk up the lane to the road, and turn right.

The entrance to **Cloud Farm** is clearly marked, follow the drive up to the farmhouse. (Author's note; excellent cream teas and home-cooked food.)

Walk down to cross the **Badgworthy Water** opposite the white-painted farmhouse and turn left upstream, following the footsteps of thousands of annual visitors who come on a pilgrimage to see the location of a novel most of them have never read, written by a man most of them have never heard of.

There is a memorial stone to R.D. Blackmore beside the path, and in the early summer the rhododendrons make this lovely valley even lovelier.

Any of the paths off to the right will lead on to **Malmsmead Hill**. That via **Lank Combe** begins immediately before the footbridge beyond a clearing. It follows the stream up what is supposed to be the water slide that features in the early chapters of Lorna Doone, although Blackmore admitted to a good deal of licence in his descriptions.

The valley of Lank Combe, which is not where the medieval village remains are to be found, is a pretty, peaceful spot. The path climbs upwards. Either keep to the stream on a very narrow path or follow the broader route which makes directly for the open moor.

The start of the valley path is at present indistinct, but perhaps if everyone leaves a stone at the junction we shall have a reasonable cairn in a few years time. Watch for a boggy depression to the left with a faint path winding through it. This is not as wet as it looks and quickly becomes a wider path, easy to follow. Turn right when the broad track comes down to ford the stream, and aim for the thorn tree, keep to its right and turn left when the main track is reached.

Walkers from **Malmsmead Hill** will join on this track.

The next signpost says Brendon, Doone valley, and Brendon Common – straight on. Bear off to the right across the heather to reach the summit of **Shilstone Hill**, complete with trig point and a fine view.

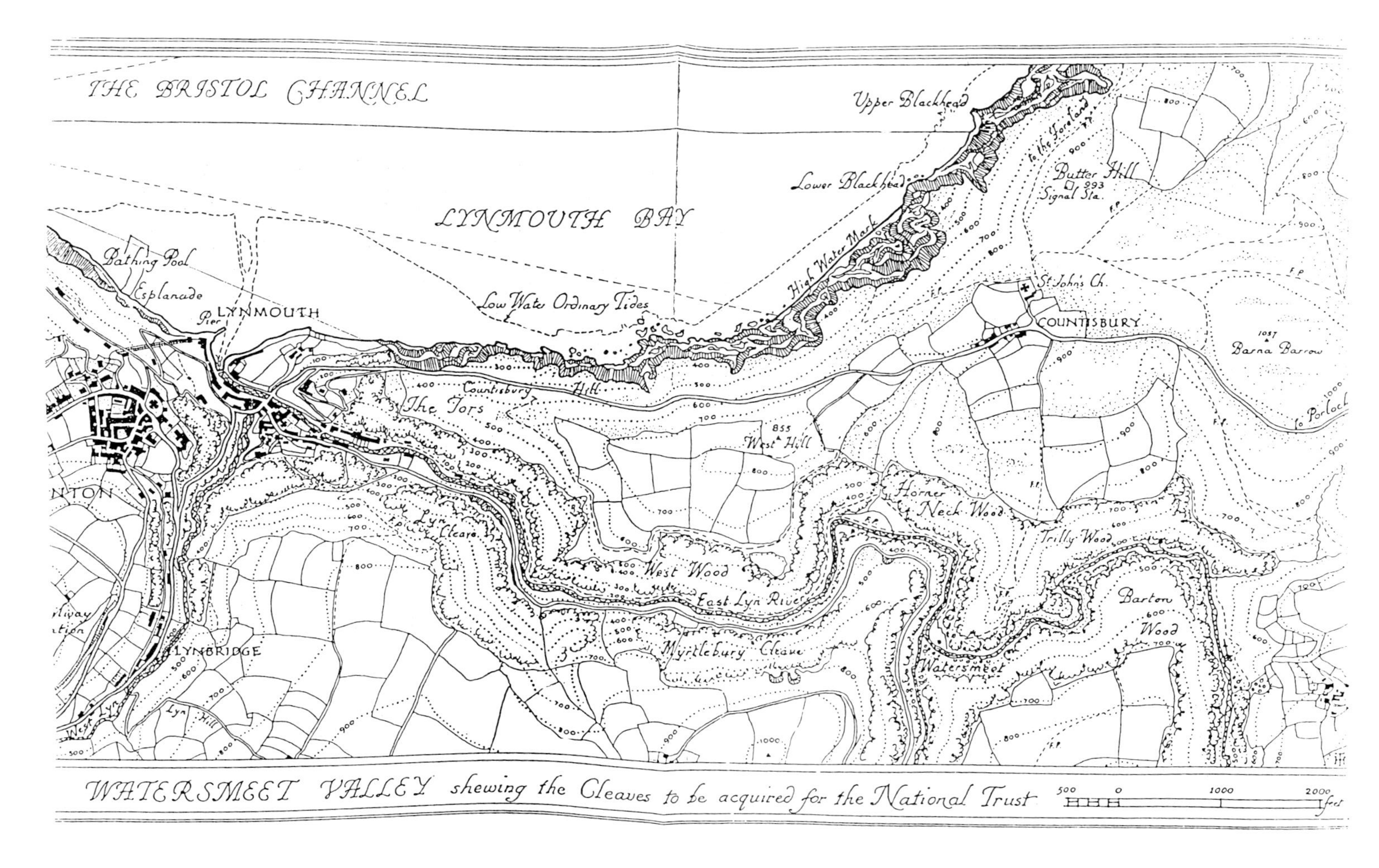

WATERSMEET VALLEY shewing the Cleaves to be acquired for the National Trust
500 0 1000 2000 feet

Follow the red marks down to cross the track; walkers from the cattle grid car park will join here; those from **Dry Bridge** will have crossed the summit of Shilstone.

The path descends via the wall and dry channel which leads down to the stream below Shilstone. There is no bridge here.

The path through the cottages and farmbuildings is marked, and keeps level across the field to the opposite hedge. Through the gap there is a fine view across the Watersmeet valley to Butter Hill. Turn downhill following the hedge and onto the lane. Downhill again and the footpath to Rockford (signposted) begins just beyond the bend.

This is the steepest section of the walk, but it is through woodland alongside a tumbling stream, and in this direction you are going downhill.

Turn left along the road to **Rockford**.

Here there is a choice of taking the short route back up via **Wilsham farm**, which is signposted from across the river, or continuing on to **Watersmeet.**

The easiest route for Watersmeet is the bridlepath, which begins the same distance again along the road beyond Rockford past the house called "Greentiles". Keep to the higher path, signposted bridlepath to Hillsford Bridge. It connects later with the lower footpath, which keeps closer to the water but has its ups and downs.

Cross the river to **Watersmeet** and continue on towards Lynmouth, taking the first path up to the right to **Countisbury** via **Chisel Combe.** (Wind Hill can be included by backtracking and crossing the field to the track).

The main road needs to be crossed with great care; the footpath around **Countisbury** to Butter Hill starts almost opposite, up a few steps and following a stone wall.

You then emerge onto the open headland once more, and follow the wall around to **Butter Hill**, the former lookout above the Foreland Point. **Barna Barrow** car park is a short stroll away. Well done!

Hollerday Hill

Distance: Around 2 miles.
Map: OS Landranger 180,
Pathfinder SS 64/74.

Some folk think that to qualify as a "decent" or "proper" walk, a respectable number of miles must be covered. This little walk proves them wrong. The same hairy-chested types also often assume that one must be far from habitation and the madding crowd. Again, wrong. Here, on the outskirts of Lynton, and sandwiched between the town and the Valley of Rocks, is a small hill, criss-crossed with paths and tracks, covered in a wide variety of vegetation, and from which there are some amazingly good views.

Hollerday Hill is correctly the preserve of the people of Lynton, and they do little to advertise the presence of such a glorious adventure ground. A path is signposted from alongside the town hall, but that is the only indication. It is an adventure ground because halfway up Hollerday Hill a wealthy Victorian and benefactor of the town built for himself a large and imposing mansion. The grounds were laid out in a series of carriage drives, walks, tennis courts and shrubberies. These all still exist – but the house was burnt down in 1913, shortly after the death of its owner. Sir George Newnes was a remarkable man. He was a publisher, responsible for the magazine "Titbits" which in his day was a serious publication. On moving to North Devon he took an active interest in the area, financing the cliff railway, built in 1890 at a cost of £8,000, and playing a major part in the building of the narrow gauge railway from Barnstaple to Lynton, which opened in 1898 and closed in 1935. It is still remembered with the nostalgic affection all such small railways seem to inspire and there is a strong movement in favour of reopening some of the line; the whole length is impossible as a reservoir has been built over part of it.

Directions

Park in Lynton and walk up the lane alongside the Town Hall.

Notice the outbuildings to the rear, presumably stables built to house the horses and cariages of the councillors. The town hall was also financed largely by Sir George Newnes – one feels there should be a statue to the fellow somewhere in the area!

Turn left uphill, following the tarmacced path, but pausing to admire the views from the gateway to the bungalow on the right.

At the first junction, turn left back over the town. This track passes Honeypot cottage, once an estate worker's dwelling, now a holiday let.

Watch for the signpost to the picnic area on the right. Follow the grassy track, but bear left before the clearing and zig zag right then left up a flight of log steps to the former tennis courts.

As with all such deserted places, the flat grassy rectangle looks both forlorn and almost haunted. Nothing happens here anymore. It has lost both its point and its purpose. It isn't even attractive.

Exit left up more log steps and turn right when the path is reached.

Turn left uphill at the signpost, and on to the summit.

Hollerday Hill is 750 feet in height and because of its isolation and proximity to the coast, has views far exceeding those expected from such an insignificant hill! It is also a very comfortable summit with plenty of grassy sitting places. On a clear day the coast of Wales is plain across the Bristol Channel, as is Lundy, and the North Devon coast in both directions, although Foreland Point blocks views eastwards. The Valley of Rocks lies below, and across the land rises to the bulk of Brendon Common and the Chains.

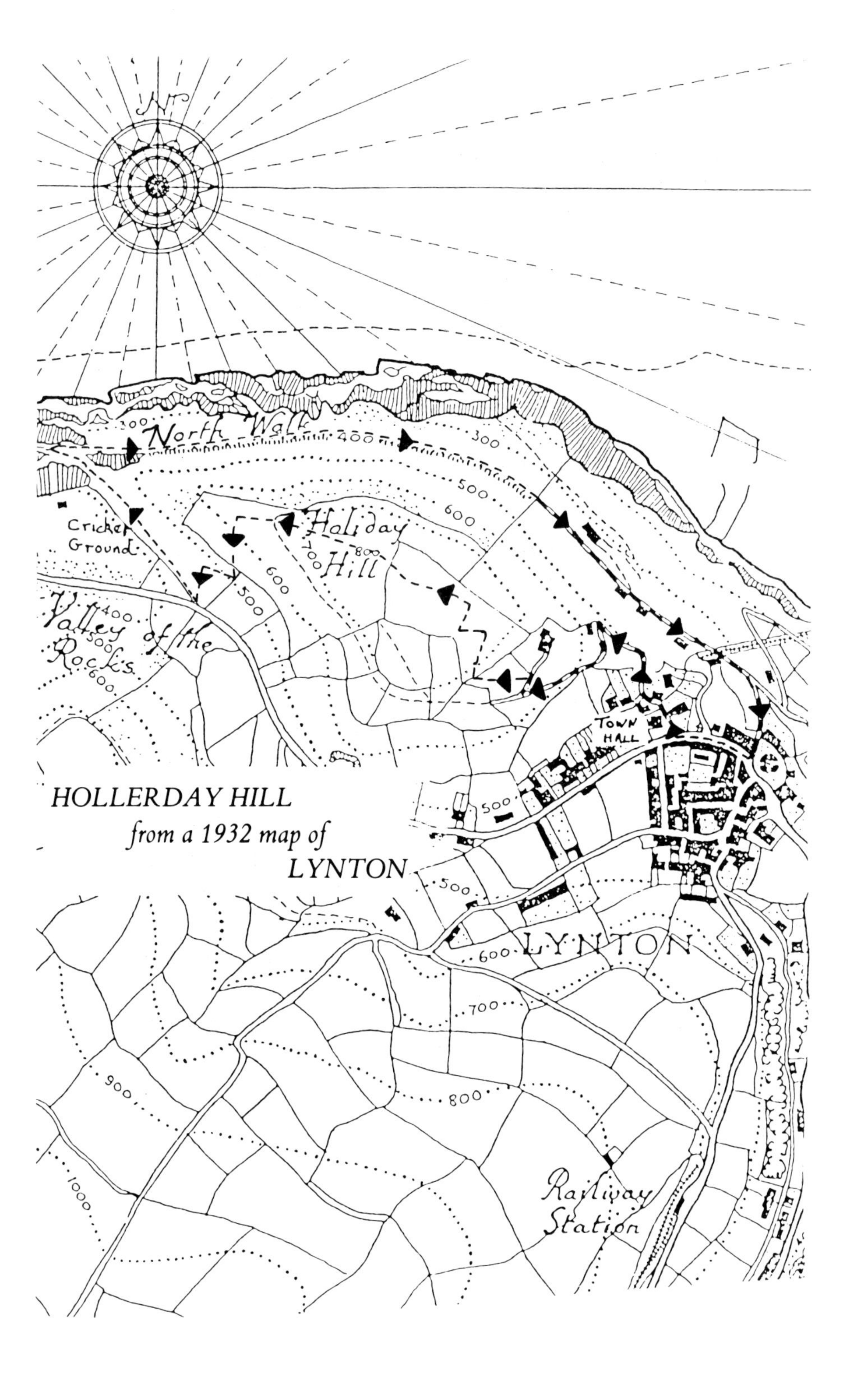
HOLLERDAY HILL
from a 1932 map of
LYNTON
North Walk
Holiday
Hill
Cricket
Ground
Valley of the
Rocks
TOWN
HALL
LYNTON
Railway
Station

Turn downhill inland from the summit alongside the ruined stone wall to meet the main path, which was left at the "picnic area" sign, (and which leads back to Lynton for those with no more time to spare).

Turn right on the path which contours round overlooking the Valley of Rocks. Ignore the coastal footpath sign which leads back too soon to Lynton, and go instead downhill to a small stonebuilt shelter.

From here there is a commanding view of the cricket pitch. Level ground of sufficient size for circket is not easily found in this hilly area of North Devon, and the slight undulations add interest to the game.

On the hillside is an elderly notice warning that those who wilfully set on **FIRE** *a wood, or coppice, trees, heath, gorse, furze or fern, constitute a* **FELONY** *and will incur severe penalties!*

This is the far point of the walk, unless an exploration of the Valley of Rocks is contemplated. Watch out for wild goats that still inhabit the ledges and crevices, and take care not to startle them.

Turn right, climbing gently uphill. The cliff top is reached and the coastal footpath leads back to Lynton, passing to seaward of Hollerday Hill. It is a level tarmacced path, cut into the sloping cliffside.

You are soon back amongst the large villas and hotels of Lynton, and the path crosses the cliff railway before returning to Lynton centre – turn right along the main centre to regain the Town Hall.

Anstey Common

The southern fringes of Exmoor have much to offer, and yet they remain strangely neglected, uncrowded and almost undiscovered. The long ridge of Anstey Common that runs down to Dulverton is familiar to all those who travel the former trunk road between South Molton and Taunton, now downgraded to B road status. The western end of the ridge is the highest, with Five Barrows Hill rising to 1,617 feet above the valley of the river Bray, and Brayford. For much of its length the old Forest of Exmoor boundary kept to this high ground, as does the county boundary between Devon and Somerset, following the road that enables motorists to enjoy some magnificent views that more energetic folk think they don't deserve!

Perhaps it is the absence of villages and inns, and the remoteness from the acknowledged centres of Exmoor that have left Anstey Common undisturbed. Yet here is some marvellous walking country with panoramic views over the Devon countryside. On a clear day the patchwork of fields stretches away towards a distant horizon; on a hazy day you get the feeling of standing on the edge of the world.

The delectable Danes Brook forms the northern boundary of the ridge, running down to the wooded banks of the river Barle. It is one of Exmoor's many minor streams that follow deep valleys, or coombes, whose tree-lined sides reach to the water's edge giving marvellous effects of light and shade, and offering many an opportunity for quiet contemplation in the dappled sunlight.

Molland is the only village of any size offering hospitality, and it is well worth a visit, although not actually on the route of the walk. The parish church contains a rare unspoilt Georgian interior, with three decker pulpit, and although the pillars of the nave lean at an alarming angle, they have been pronounced safe! Next door is the London Inn, an ancient and hospitable inn known not only for its excellent ale and food, but also for the collection of cats and birds. At the time of writing it is still a genuine "local" untouched by the fell hand of the giant breweries. Long may it continue.

A word of warning is needed; the footpath starting behind the inn leading to Smallacombe farm (clearly shown on the OS map) is very far from clear under foot. It can be found; it is unobstructed but so rarely used that it takes some patient searching for, especially the footbridge across the stream.

An unfenced road runs along the summit of the ridge of Anstey Common, and there are several parking places adjacent to the cattle grids, so that non-walking members of the party can be left looking at the views. These parking areas also mean that the walk can have a number of starting points and several permutations in the way of figure of eights, or shortened versions. The walk is a delight from start to finish in whichever direction it is undertaken, and the only steep section is the lane leading down to the Danes Brook.

Start Point

The three best parking areas are Anstey Gate, Woodland Corner, or down by Danes Brook where there is limited car parking, with the advantage of shade.

Directions

From **Woodland Common** (most convenient from the former A361); park off the lane to the left of the cattlegrid.

Take the footpath across the moor almost opposite the junction, and signposted "Hawkridge 2½". A lone pine tree on the right makes a distinctive feature, and here the moor is heather covered.

The summit road across Anstey Common is soon reached. (Here is another possible parking area). Cross this and bend right to join the broad track, which follow for a short distance until a narrow footpath bears off to the left.

Distance: Around 5 miles.
Maps: OS Landranger 180.
Pathfinder SS 82/92.

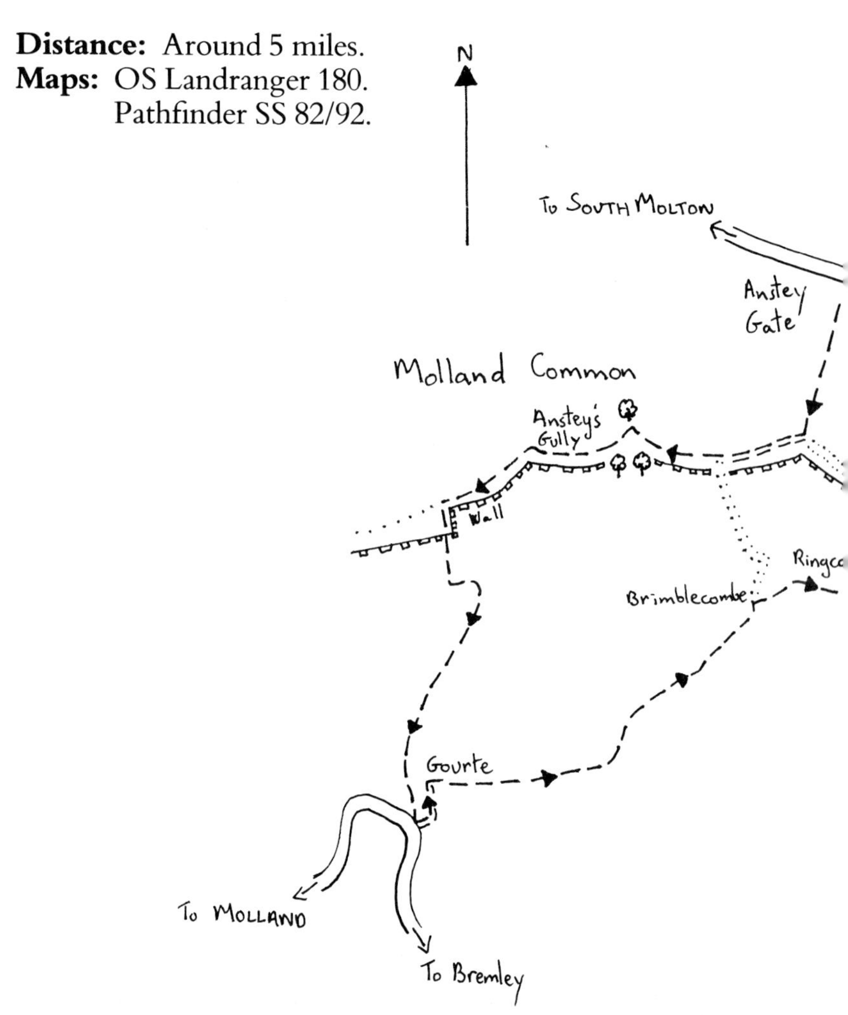

Past the steep gully, look for a path down to the left. The "gravestone" on the left marks the limit of Venfordland. The path ends suddenly on the steep lane down to Danes Brook, which forms the boundary between the parishes of Hawkridge and West Anstey, as the marker stone in the centre of Slade bridge testifies. It is also the county boundary, but this is of less importance! Here is a delectable spot, with trees lining the banks and the broadening stream making pools and shallows fringed by shingle beaches. A place to linger.

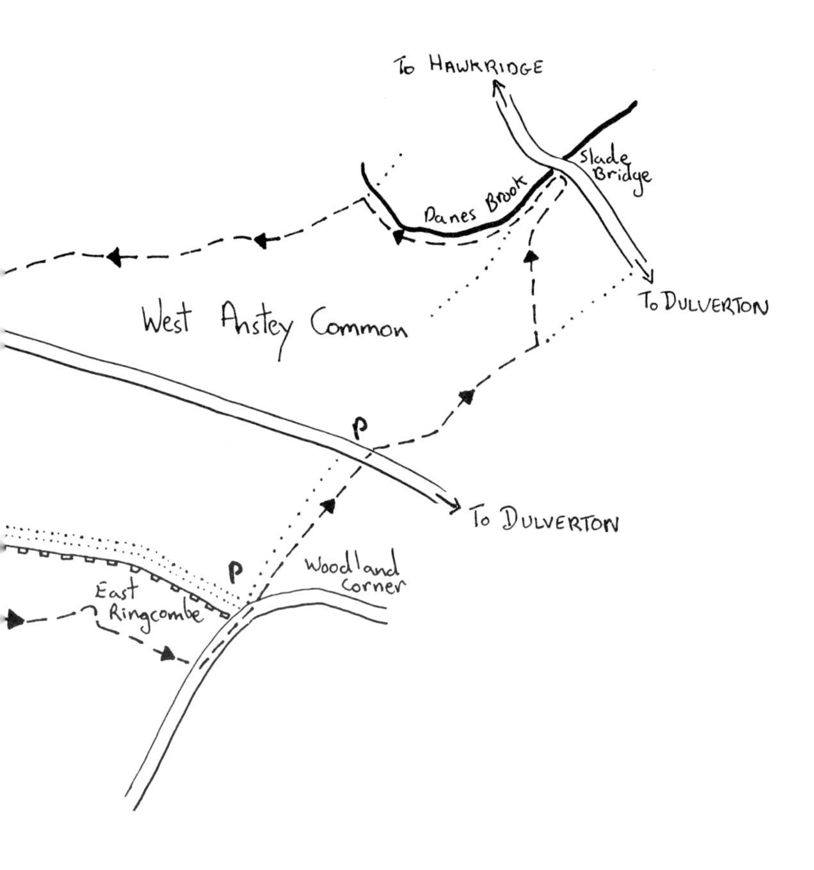

A "permissive footpath" follows the lefthand bank upstream, beginning immediately adjoining the parapet of the bridge, between two trees. Keep to the stream as closely as possible.

After a short distance a path ascends to the left. This avoids the grassy areas which can be marshy and returns to the river bank. After crossing a stream it can be followed back to the summit road, the shortest version of this walk, but worthwhile nonetheless.

Continue along the riverbank to the ford. The signpost pointing back downstream says "Alternative scenic riverside path to Slade Bridge", presumably an alternative for when the ford (the route to Hawkridge) is impassable.

Here turn left uphill, taking your leave of the Danes Brook. There are a number of paths and tracks, but all lead diagonally upwards across the common to the ridge road, and Anstey Gate.

The trees clothing the valley of the Danes Brook make a grand view, especially in autumn, perhaps the best time for this walk.

Anstey Gate

A possible start point, the nearest to Molland and with the best views.

There are two options. By turning left immediately beyond the gate, an unmistakeable track leads gently downhill – the route to Brimblecombe gate.

The alternative is the bridlepath that begins by following the direction of the road before crossing the moor to join the boundary path from Anstey's Gully. This area of common is crossed with several tracks and paths, some of which peter out, and the ground can be very wet and boggy. Under these conditions the driest, surest path is along the wall.

This meets the unsurfaced road from Woodland Corner (a quick return route).

Turn right and the farm entrance to Brimblecombe is soon reached. (This provides another short cut back to Woodland Corner.)

The full circuit of the walk continues along the path to Anstey's Gully. The hedge here marks the division between open moorland and cultivated farmland. Anstey's Gully is a lovely wooded valley with a stoney gorge, dry in its highest reaches except in very wet weather, and reminiscent of limestone country. There are several of these dry gullys in this area, a rarity on Exmoor.

Follow the hedge and after another lesser dip, watch for a metal gate in the angle of the wall, which is not signposted, but the marks of horses hooves are an indicator. Follow the track around the field, then downhill along the ridge, a lovely path and marked a bridleway at its far end.

Here turn left and follow the lane to Gourte Farm. The stoney track passes the farm and rises between high banks and out into a field.

Take the gateway into the wood to the right and follow the path down through the conifers to the ford. This is almost always wet, but by keeping to the right you will find the next best thing to dry ground.

At Brimblecombe keep the farmhouse on your right and follow the track uphill. A gap in the bank just above the farm is the start of the path to Ringcombe, the next farm along the ridge. (The track, if followed, will rejoin the track from Woodland Corner at the point where the path from Anstey Gate comes down.)

The path to Ringcombe is not well used but there are no difficulties. It contours along the valley side, with views across to Combe Wood and makes a pleasing, more domesticated contrast to the untamed moorland.

At Ringcombe the path again passes behind the farm and comes down onto the farm road by a magnificent holly tree.

Look for the path across the road. This leads down to a small stream (no bridge) with a gate across it, then ascends the bank beyond. Again, the path is not well used, and again passes behind the buildings of East Ringcombe Farm before coming down to the farm track.

Turn right along this and follow the farm road to the lane, then left and back to the car at Woodland Corner.

Trentishoe & Heddon's Cleave

Distance: Around 4 miles.
Maps: OS Landranger 180,
Pathfinder SS 64/74.
NT Leaflets "Combe Martin & The Great Hangman" and "Heddon Valley & Woody Bay".

Within a relatively small area here is some of the best walking country that North Devon has to offer. This is hidden country, unsuspected by the tourists and coach parties who make Heddon's Mouth a noisy, clamorous place in the season. It is also neglected by many visitors to Exmoor for whom it is just too far from the centre of things, and difficult to reach down narrow country lanes. If they read this book, they'll know they are missing something, but there should be room for all of us.

There will be many visitors who are content to stroll down to Heddon's Mouth from the Hunters Inn car park, look at the beach, and stroll back. Until I started exploring I thought Heddon's Mouth had little else to offer, but how wrong I was, and this walk has rapidly become one of my favourites, offering a dramatic section of the coastal footpath, the only steep scree slope in North Devon, and woodland of a quiet sylvan beauty unsuspected by the thousands who park in the valley below. Those who walk quietly may well be rewarded by the sighting of deer.

Study the map carefully to decide how far you want to walk. Holdstone Down is an added option, but by climbing to its summit, the walker gains a terrific feeling of superiority for he has been to the highest point along this coast, which amazingly is by-passed by the coastal footpath! The views gained are considerable and well worth the very minimal effort.

Possible car parks

For the longest walk and the car park with the best views, use the Holdstone Down car park, which is signposted on the road from Combe Martin.

Alternatives are the area by the bungalows further on, or the car park overlooking the sea just short of Holdstone Down Cross, where the road for Trentishoe Church branches to the left.

The main path to the summit of Holdstone Down is evident from the last two car parks.

Directions

From **Holdstone Down** car park;

Follow the path from the car park, leaving on the left, which climbs upwards to the small quarry, then up again to the summit, which is not in view until the last moment. At 1,146 feet, this is the highest point on the North Devon coast. Only Barna Barrow at Foreland Point is higher, from which the views are nowhere near as impressive, and which is not truly on the coastline.

Bear right from the summit, descending down the broad but stony path to the bungalows.

At one time a grand design was envisaged with a bungalow development spreading out from the road; fortunately it never grew beyond what you can see; but some of the strange markings on the ground are now explained.

Cross the road and take the path to the left, signposted Trentishoe Mill (site of).

The path is unmistakeable. Follow the yellow mark to the left, and keep to the left through the area of young birches. The path descends steeply to join the Ladies Mile path between Trentishoe Manor and the road at Rhydda Bank Cross.

The path is sheer delight, except when rendered difficult underfoot through wet weather and too much equestrian use. The intriguingly named Ladies Mile path is presumably a relict of the days when Trentishoe Manor was owned by the squire and this walk was made as a gentle stroll for his lady; I can't believe she was expected to walk to church in her Sunday best!

Turn left along the Ladies Mile, crossing a stile. Below is the river valley, and all around is a lightly wooded area, with rhododendrons, bluebells, primroses and young birches, some showing signs of damage, presumably from deer. The path contours round the bulk of Trentishoe Down, brooding above you to the left.

At the first junction, turn down to the right. A path comes down from the Holdstone Down Cross car park and it will be seen that this walk is much better this way round, for it is a steep climb up by either route over Trentishoe Down.

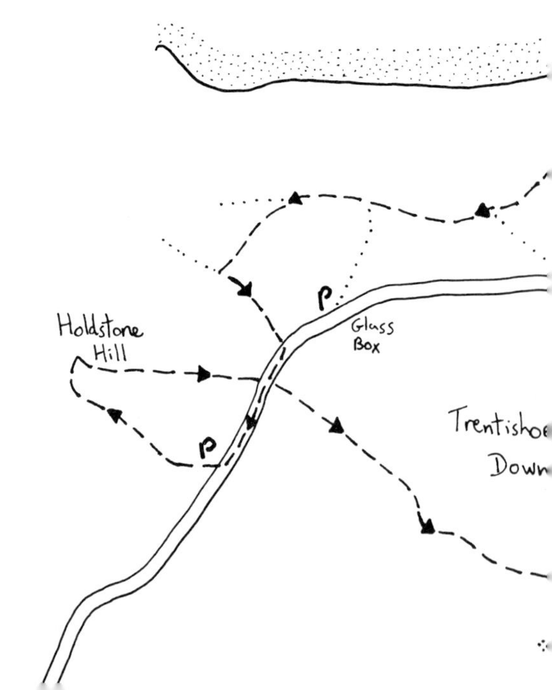

At the junction there is a copper beech, a group of rowans, and wild raspberries in summer. It is also possible to view Heale Brake across the valley, and decide whether to include it in the walk, or give it a miss.

On reaching the lane (to Trentishoe Manor) turn left for a short distance, then take the track to the right, signposted to Heale and the Hunters Inn. If Heale Brake is not to be included, continue down this path to the road.

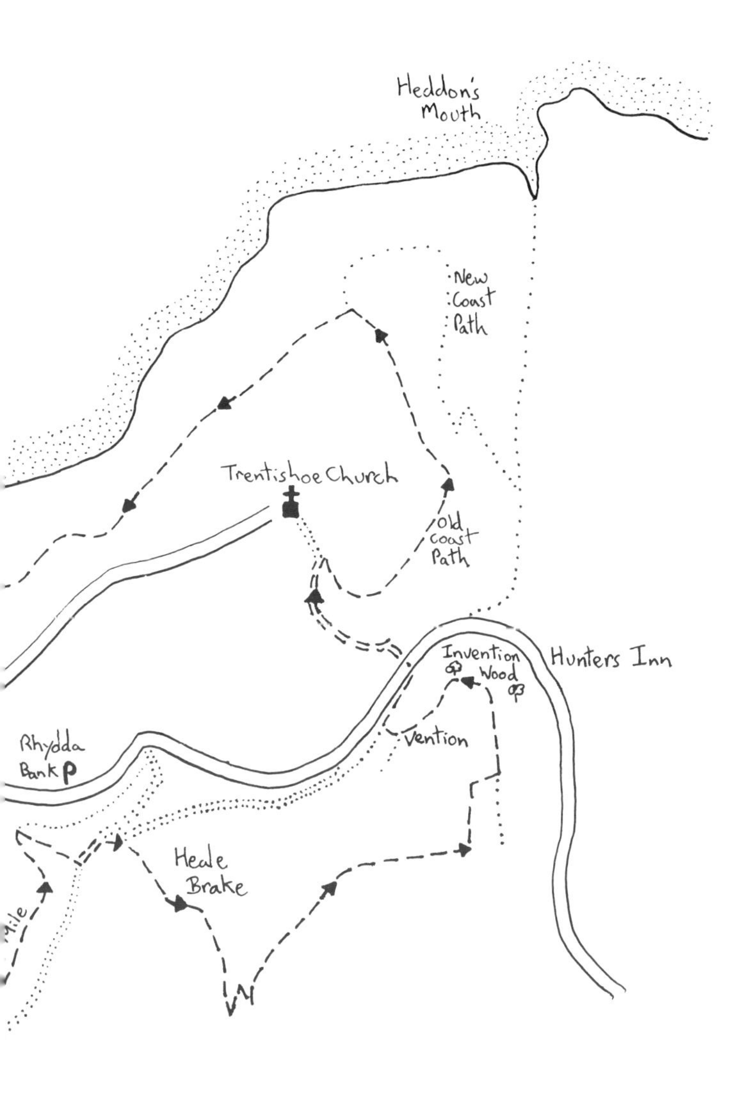

It is not necessary to climb Heale Brake, and this will add perhaps an hour to the walk; the climb is moderate, away from the crowds, and it is here in Black Cleave and Invention Wood that I usually sight deer. From the summit there is a perfect cameo view of Heddon's Cleave, and as one descends, the carbound hordes parked in the valley can be viewed with lofty disdain.

For **Heale Brake,** turn right to cross the footbridge with a stile and gate on the far side of the stream, and follow the path upwards, bearing left. It climbs through a marshy woodland, but keep to the left of the stream and a track becomes clear.

The opposite hillside is worn in strange, parallel ledges, the action of wind and frost. In spring it is one mass of primroses.

The path curves through two gates to emerge on a farm lane; turn left and follow the track into a field above the woods. Keep the beech hedge on your right until it meets a ruined wall with evidence of a former hedge. Turn left before the wall, following a newly made track separated from the field by wire fencing.

Straight ahead is Heddon's Cleave, framed by the steep-sided valley slopes. To the right in the valley below is the Hunter's Inn. The original, much smaller, inn was thatched but was burnt down in 1895 and rebuilt as we see it today.

Continue downhill through the woods, bearing round to the left.

At "Vention cottage" continue down to cross the stream, and turn right down hill, to **rejoin the route**.

On reaching the road, turn right, then left uphill on a grassy lane signposted "unsuitable for motors" which is not entirely true.

An old sign indicates that this was the original coastal footpath, and watch for the sign before the church that turns right towards the sea. It is still, in the opinion of the author, the best alternative. The newer option starts from the Heddon's Mouth valley route and climbs quite sharply up the valley side. A path has been cut around the Peter Rock, but this has no advantage over the original as the mouth itself cannot be seen, the path is narrow and the cliff falls steeply away, giving anxious moments to those who do not like the sensation of walking above a precipice.

Turn right on the pleasant grassy path that winds around the valley from Trentishoe church lane, which is a delight, and it is difficult to see why anyone should wish to cut a new path to replace it.

Follow this round, with its excellent views down into the valley, giving a bird's eye view of the paths on the opposite side of the cleave.

Continue around and wait for the sudden views westward along the coast taking in the Great Hangman, Combe Martin and the cliffs beyond. Here the new path joins.

The coastal path is easy to follow, with only one awkward section at present where erosion has forced the path to the field side of the boundary.

The path crosses a field, then divides; turn sharply left uphill to the Holdstone Down Cross car park, or continue on the coastal path.

Turn left uphill for the middle car park, and left back up to the bungalows, which can be seen, along "Seaview Road". To reach Holdstone Down car park, turn right along the road.

The Great Hangman

There are two direct routes to the Great Hangman summit, one very easy and one for the more energetic. A third route skirts Holdstone Down and Sherrycombe, picking up the coastal footpath to climb the steep slopes of the Hangman. If there is a driver available to meet you at Combe Martin, then this last choice makes a grand one-way walk.

Circular walks can be worked out for all three, but they all involve some road work, and in particular the return to Combe Martin via Girt Down involves narrow lanes with the typical high hedges so effective in blocking out the views. My recommendation is to return by the same route, unless transport is available.

The paths are generally good and dry underfoot. There is no shelter anywhere, and the cliffs here are very exposed. Only those who relish battling with the elements and enjoy the sensation of being blown off their feet, should venture on this walk when there are strong winds. It is likewise dangerous in misty conditions. But when the weather is settled and visibility good, then this is a marvellous walk.

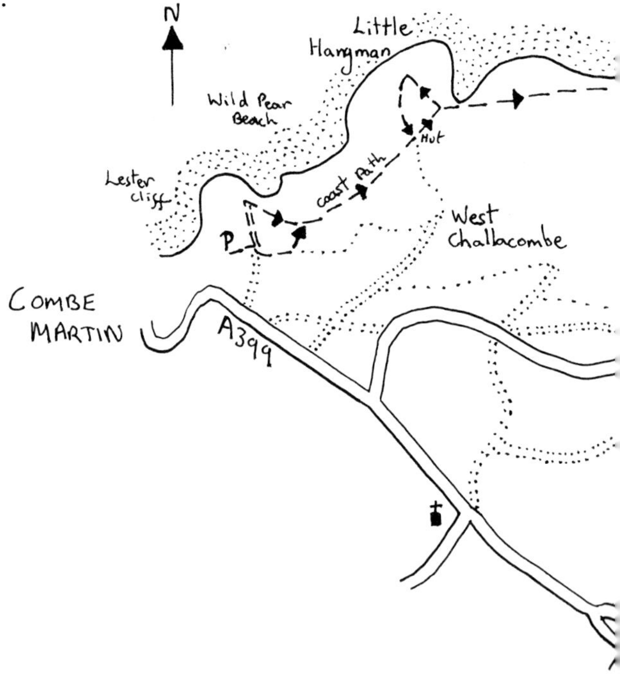

Distance: Variable, from 1 mile to 4½ miles.
Maps: OS Landranger 180,
Pathfinder SS 64/74.
NT Leaflet "Combe Martin and the Great Hangman".

Directions
From **Combe Martin**

Use the large car park overlooking Combe Martin beach and harbour.

The official coast path is signposted and follows a narrow lane to the right of the residential road serving the houses above the car park. Behind them the path turns seawards and reaches a sturdy shelter built close to the cliff edge.

An alternative path leaves the car park at the far end of the grassy slope and climbs steeply to Lester Point. It is slippery after rain.

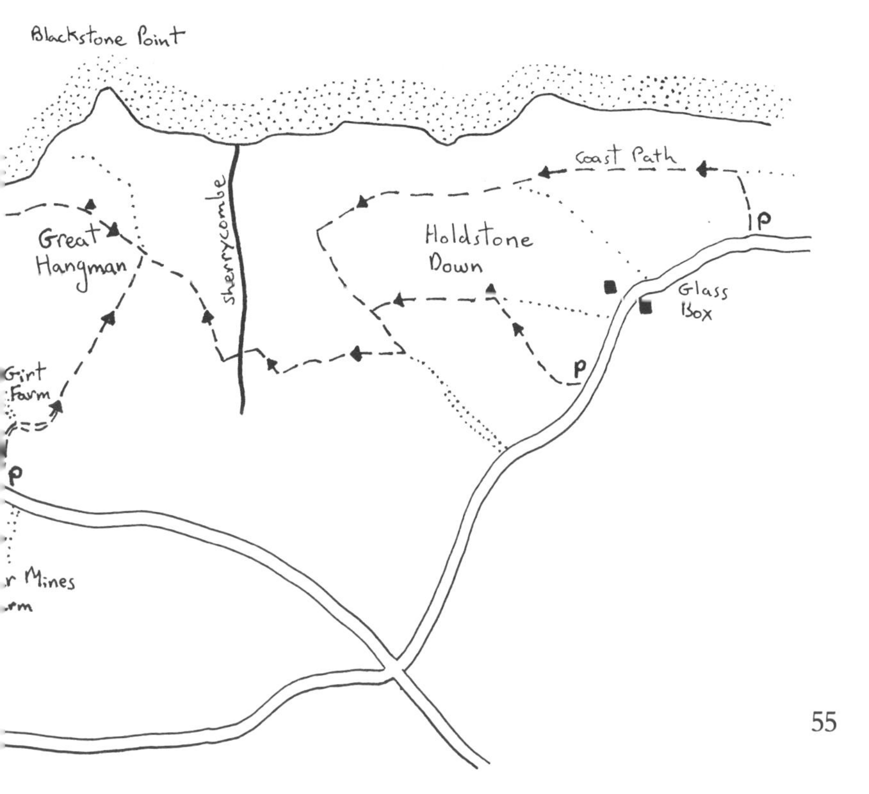

Wild Pear Beach lies, far, far below, too far if the Great Hangman is the objective.

An unexpected sight is the cafe alongside the footpath. Wild Pear beach is popular in the summer and the cafe must be a welcome oasis for thirsty walkers and beach-goers alike.

The path ascends gently towards the Little Hangman, which is best left for the return journey when it is reached with much less effort.

The path continues, well trodden all the way to the Great Hangman summit.

At over 1,000 feet above sea level, the Great Hangman is the second highest point along the North Devon coast, and could justifiably claim the title of 'mountain'. And it is literally above sea level, for below its domed summit the wild seas of the Bristol Channel break upon an invisible shore. Were it not for the nature of the cliffs, traditionally described as 'hog's back', sloping steeply to terminate in low cliffs some 150 feet high, the summit of the Hangman would be a dizzy eyrie.

The origins of the name are uncertain but geologists prefer the corruption of An Maen, Hill of Stone, to the doubtful stories about sheep stealers hanging themselves by accident, or the quite possible siting of the gallows in medieval times.

The summit cairn is a rarity in North Devon.

"Viewpoint". Only those with a very good head for heights should be tempted to venture along the narrow path that winds across the breast of the Hangman. This originally led to silver mines that delved far into the heart of the mountain. Some of the old workings could only be reached by sea, making it a doubly hazardous way of earning a living.

Return by the same route; the views are better in reverse. The land falls away in a great sweep before levelling, and rising to the shapely height of the Little Hangman. Although only 716 feet, this lesser summit far exceeds its big brother as a view point. It is also well endowed with pleasant grassy platforms and ledges which invite repose and the opportunity for leisurely appreciation of Combe Martin and the cliffs beyond. Were it not for its extra feet, the Great Hangman would not compare at all, for it must be said it is a comfortless, exposed spot!

From **Girt Down**

Parking

Leave the car at the entrance of Girt Farm, and follow the signposted track to the cliffs, and the Great Hangman. No problems and very little effort required.

From **Holdstone Down**

Use either of the car parks specified in the Trentishoe Walk.

Either ascend Holdstone Down, by far the best choice, or walk back to the path signposted from the road which leads to Sherrycombe.

Here the coastal footpath is joined, which follow around the combe and up to the Hangman. This is a well trodden path with no problems, and keeps well clear of the cliff edge.

Sherrycombe is a steep dramatic cleft, terminating in a waterfall visible only from the sea. Exploration is best left to scramblers and climbers only.

The return route can be varied by keeping to the coastal path, which keeps to the seaward side of Holdstone Down, and follow Seaview Road back to the bungalows and the car parks.

Bull Point

Between the two villages of Mortehoe and Lee there lies a peninsula of hilly ground bounded by two narrow lanes and the sea. It contains a few farms, one of great antiquity, Bull Point lighthouse, and little else. The coastal scenery is superb; steep folds and contortions have created a series of deep valleys and steep hillsides where it is possible to wander all day out of sight of civilisation – and often out of sight of other mortals.

It also undeniably makes for strenuous walking, and between Mortehoe and Lee there are four major climbs to be taken into account. To some, an added attraction that would lead to greater popularity were the area accessible by car, is the access to the shoreline. At Rockham there is a sandy beach, and at two other points rocky inlets offer the possibility of at least a paddle.

Mortehoe village contains everything necessary. There is a free car park opposite the petrol station, with public conveniences, three inns, a cafe and take-away, plus several shops. There is also an ancient church said to contain many interesting features with a largely unspoilt interior dating from Norman times, but as it is kept locked these will have to be taken as read! Until Woolacombe was developed in the nineteenth century, Mortehoe was the centre for the area with the village school and church for the parish. Its inhabitants gained a living either from the sea, collecting limpets and edible seaweed, or the land. There was also a strong tradition of smuggling. Now totally eclipsed by its larger neighbour, and bypassed by the road to Ilfracombe, it has never developed much beyond its original limits.

The valley of **Lee** is long and sheltered and renowned for its mild climate in which all kinds of subtropical plants flourish with a luxuriance unknown elsewhere. The village has developed in two sections. The former fishing community is down by the shore and half a mile inland are the Grampus Inn and post office, with houses spread out along the valley. Currently, there is no parking at the seaward end, and only a small area in the higher village. From the map it would appear to be immaterial whether the walk is begun at Lee or Mortehoe, but it makes a very great difference on the ground. From one who has walked it in both directions, by far the best choice is to begin at Mortehoe, where the parking is considerably easier. Not only are the three flights of steps all down, but the views are better, with the sweep of Rockham Bay round to Bull Point, and then along the coast as far as Ilfracombe. The view opens before you as you walk, whereas in the other direction it is barred by the next height to be scaled – a daunting prospect.

There are several permutations given for the return walk. The footpath shown on the map via Damage Barton is included, but not recommended. The start via Borough valley is fine, walking through woodland, but the climb up to the road is very steep and the path from there on is indistinct. Damage Barton is worth a visit, but it is sad to see such ancient farm buildings falling into decay. Grouped around a courtyard are a range of slatebuilt barns and shippens, a former mill and a ruinous farmhouse, dating from at least 1650, and as recently as 1950 still in fair repair. The barton itself was a medieval mansion, the one-time owners becoming lords of the manor of Lee.

Easewell Farm is now a well organised camp site and the footpath passes through the middle between the swimming pool and farmhouse, past the shop and toilet block and through the tents and caravans!

Infinitely to be preferred is the peaceful route via Wrinkle Wood.

Distance: At least 3 miles.
Maps: OS Landranger 180,
Pathfinder SS 44/54.
NT Leaflet 'Ilfracombe to Woolacombe'

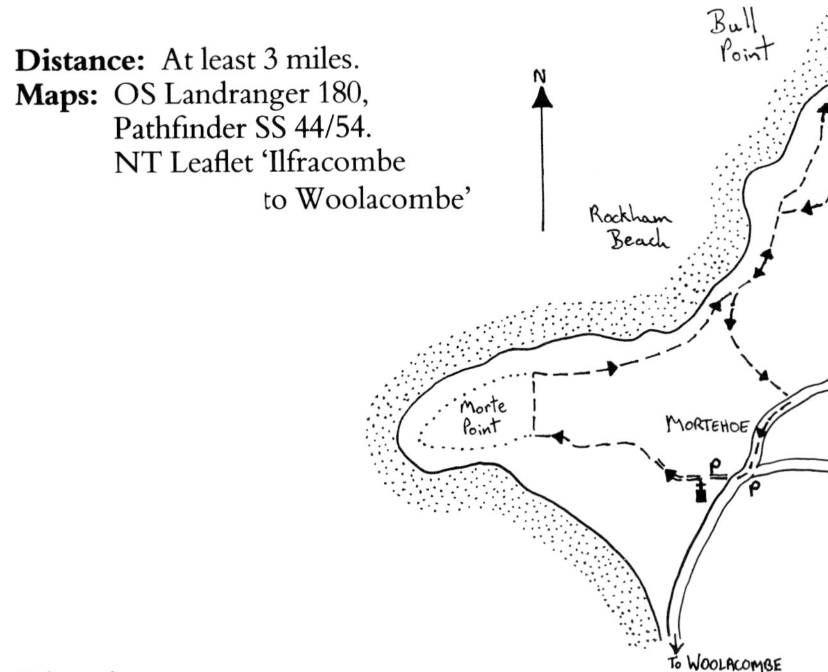

Directions

Park in Mortehoe and locate the lane between the church and the "Ship Aground" public house.

Follow the lane past the cemetery and out onto the open headland of Morte Point, through the gates proclaiming it to be a Memorial Park.

The whole headland is worth exploring, and a path follows the cliff edge with several seats and benches. Detailed expoloration could be left until the completion of the walk so that less energetic members can sit and admire the view whilst others scramble among the slates. Off the Point is the Morte Stone – the death stone! It is claimed that the Normans gave this name to the rocks off Morte Point around which the seas ceaselessly break. Whether they did or not, its name has been all too apt for many a poor sailor. Five ships foundered in one winter (1852) alone, and it is still a major hazard although now marked by a warning buoy and the flashing light of Bull Point lighthouse.

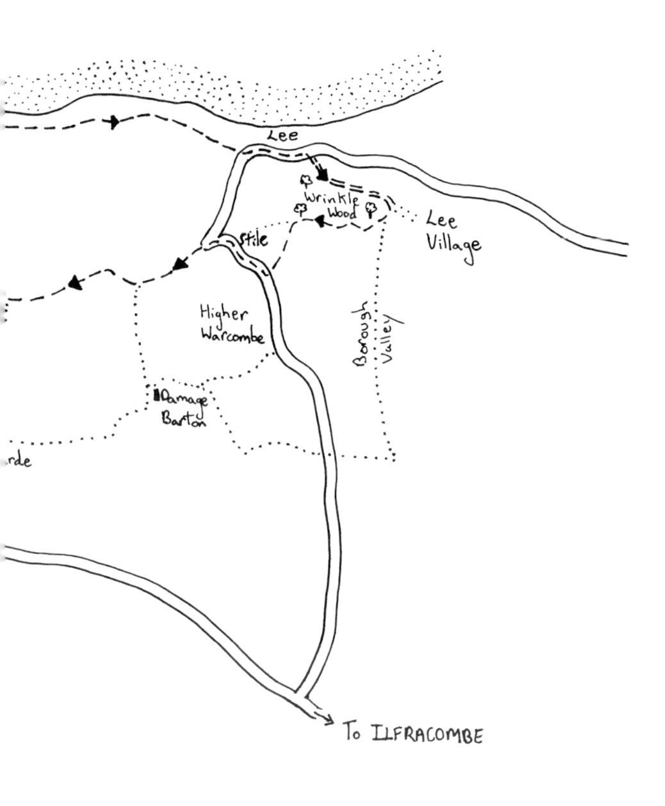

The geology of the area is interesting, and the rocks that make up Morte Point and the surrounding cliffs are known as Morte Slates. They have an almost luminous quality, being pale grey and shiny, and when wet are very slippery. Erosion has exposed large areas on Morte Point where the sharp upturned edges give the landscape a surrealist air and make for uncomfortable sitting!

Most of the cliffs are now owned by the National Trust, but in 1910 the story was very different as shown by this account in "The Coastal Scenery of North Devon" by E A Newell Arber.

'From Bull Point to Rockham Beach there is no way along the cliffs which is not a trespass, and it may be necessary to make a long detour, following the carriage road from the Lighthouse to

North Morte, whence there is a footpath to Rockham Beach. There is a path to the shore here, but the coast can only be explored for a very limited distance to the North or South.

The next promontory, Morte Point, has recently been bought and consecrated to the use of the general public, and, as a natural consequence, some of the approaches are now fenced in with formidable iron railings. There is no way from Rockham Bay to Morte Point, except by returning by the path, above mentioned, to North Morte, and then by the road to Morthoe Church, where a fenced path begins which leads to the promontory.'

From the gate, follow the path downwards alongside a low stone wall. Turn right when the lighthouse can be seen, walking past a wooden seat and a small spring to join the coast path. The first flight of steps – 59 of them, leads down to the valley from North Morte.

A gentle incline, then another steep descent, 68 steps, down to Rockham beach. There are more steps down to the beach itself.

The coastal footpath climbs up to the rocky knoll ahead, but a gentler variation leads around the base to meet the path, which has turned right on top of the knoll. Follow the path to the lighthouse.

Bull Point lighthouse was originally built in 1897, but what you see today is the newest light in the country. The original was severely damaged by a landslip in 1972 when 50 feet of cliff crashed into the sea. The present lighthouse was completed by 1974 and has a modern keeper's bungalow to go with it. It is open to the public in the afternoons, subject to the keeper's availability.

Continue on the coast path, descending to the small valley at Damagehue, where there is a rocky cove.

Another ascent, another headland, and one last steep descent (39 steps) to another rocky cove. Two stiles with dog gates have to be negotiated. These dog gates in the stiles are a feature of the National Trust – owned coastal paths, and are a very great help to owners of large dogs. Let us hope the idea catches on.

One final ascent, without steps which I find a tedious imposition on the walker, to the final headland.

The small sandy cove, Hilly Mouth, can be reached via a steep flight of wooden steps. An older flight cut into the rock leads down on the far side. The start is no longer clear but they are an interesting reminder of the lengths people would go to in the pursuit of earning a living (legal or otherwise) from the sea. They must have been hazardous and often slippery, especially when carrying heavy and cumbersome baskets.

This headland for a short time was laid out as Lee golf course. It lasted from 1904 until the Second World War – and must have required a high degree of skill from the players.

The path descends to the road and down to Lee.

A handful of former fishermen's cottages line the shore, that on the far side was the manor mill and retained its mill wheel until comparatively recently. The large hotel was built in the early 1900s, replacing the original manorhouse on the same site, which had been rebuilt high above on the hillside.

The footpath turns right inland before the hotel, beginning on a tarmacced road used by the buses, and which used to lead to a large car park.

The footpath rejoins the road higher up which can be followed if the rest of Lee is to be explored. The Grampus inn is a short distance away.

Turn right immediately in front of the stone wall (signposted) below the large house, and before reaching the road.

Cross the stream. The footpath immediately divides: the first instructions are for the **Wrinkle Wood** route.

Do not turn left, but carry on uphill, signposted footpath to Higher Warcombe. There is a steep pull up to the manor house through cool woodland in which there are some fine copper beeches and carpets of bluebells and primroses.

Cross the drive to the short flight of steps opposite. The path continues through woodland to emerge into a field.

Again there is a choice. By bearing left, and then right to pick up the path under the electricity wire, the path leads to the road and ***Higher Warcombe*** *farm. The path to* ***Damage Barton*** *begins beyond the gate marked Warcombe Cottage and leads complicatedly through the farm buildings, indicated by yellow arrows. Cross the field and pass through two wooden posts, then aim for the roofs of the farmbuildings and a pile of discarded building blocks.*

Bear right, around the scrub, then left on a faint track and aim for the gate and stile on the far side. These lead onto the lane down to Lee.

Turn right downhill and follow the lane until the sharp right hand bend, where the path is signposted to the left.

Follow the path to its junction with a farm track where there are four gates. Take the higher of the two right hand gates, marked Bull Point, although the u, p, o and t are missing so that a quick glance gives the impression of a bull in the field!

Watch for the stile on the left before the open headland is reached (signposted). Cross the field and descend through a small wood carpetted with spring flowers, to the stream. Follow this down to the junction with the path from the lighthouse road.

For everyone that slavishly follows the coastal path, very few discover the delights of this lovely area, only a stone's throw away.

Another choice; the quickest route back is to turn left and follow the lighthouse road back to Mortehoe.

Turn right downhill and at the fork climb left uphill to reach the lighthouse road. Follow this for a short distance, through the cutting, then watch for a track off to the left.

Walk down across the field towards what looks like a mine chimney, but take the gate on the right then continue downhill. The chimney is actually a beautifully constructed slate column that once supported the roof of some agricultural building, long defunct.

The coastal path at Rockham is rejoined at the bottom. Follow this towards Morte up the first ascent only, and at the top, beyond the stile, bear left through the scrub. The path quickly becomes an easily graded, tarmacced path and allelujah! Mortehoe is in sight! Turn right on reaching the village road back to the car park.

Return through **Borough Valley.**

From **Lee** follow the footpath as far as the stream, then turn left signposted to Borough.

The wooded valley is a good example of neglected woodland. The trees are sparse, ivyhung and undergrown with vigorous brambles. The far side is now a conifer plantation.

Climb up to the parish road and cross to the stile opposite. Cross the field (which may be ploughed) to a stile in the opposite hedge.

Bear right through the gorse and aim for the gate. (In reverse keep to the left hand edge of the field).

The path now becomes indistinct but aim for a wet, boggy area and you are on course. Negotiate this and pick up the track beyond it which leads via a large dump of unwanted wire netting down to Damage Barton. Here the path from Higher Warcombe is joined.

Pass through the farm buildings and follow the farm drive, looking for the start of the path to Yarde and Easewell farms, and thence to Mortehoe. This is easy to follow and marked with yellow arrows.

Torrington Common

Most walks in North Devon concentrate on the coast, or on that part of Exmoor that lies within the county boundary. Until very recently the hinterland was largely ignored by tourism, everything being geared to beaching and fishing villages etc. etc. But things are looking slightly different now, with more inland attractions opening every year and the tourist boards turning their attention away from the coast, for which good weather is needed for best enjoyment, to other pursuits and a wider variety.

Torrington is a former market town with a long history. It reached the height of its prosperity in the days of the woollen industry, as did most of Devon, and its long decline was only halted by the "milk factory", now part of Unigate down by the river Torridge, North Devon Meat factory, a huge abbatoir and meat processing plant exporting meat all over the world, and the Dartington glass factory.

It is surprising that the natural beauties of Torrington's position have yet to be exploited. Nothing in the town gives any indication of the magnificent views and the fine walks, nor does the OS map give any hint of the delights in store for the explorer with "viewpoint" marks.

The whole of Castle Hill is laid out with good, surfaced paths criss-crossing from the top, where there are seats a plenty, down to the river bank. It was laid out in the nineteenth century and the obelisk at the far end commemorates the battle of Waterloo. From here there are views towards Rosemoor, the town's latest attraction in the form of several acres of beautiful gardens now in the ownership of the Royal Horticultural Society.

To find this area, aim for the Castle Hill car park, and simply walk out onto the hilltop.

At the other end of the town is Torrington Common, 365 acres of open countryside, covered with bracken and birch trees and recently the subject of some rather forced "landscaping" in the form of a series of ponds along the valley bottom. A golf course occupies most of Furzebeam Hill, but it is still common ground and from here there are magnificent views down the valley of the Torridge, looking towards Bideford.

Start Point

A large car parking area is situated on the edge of the town, before the cemetery, and is provided with children's swings, toilets, an excellent food wagon, and an icecream van most of the year. Many people come here just for an afternoon out, and never stir far from their car.

Even without directions most walker's will manage to enjoy themselves, but the walk described takes in the best points of the common.

Directions

From the car park follow the track downhill by the stone wall and beech trees that borders the cemetery.

Turn right, following the wall. Continue on the path which begins to descend into the valley down a series of steps to a timber bridge crossing the stream. Here it performs a most marked series of double loops, which will surely disappear within the next decade, so narrow is the isthmus between the banks.

The prominent factory building is Dartington Glass. This opened in 1968 with a largely Swedish workforce and was funded by the Dartington enterprise based near Totnes, in South Devon, which aims to encourage rural pursuits, although the factory can hardly be described as a cottage industry. It is now very big business and continually expands, and has a cafeteria, two "seconds" shops and huge car parks. The conducted tours of the factory are very popular.

Distance: At least 2½ miles.
Maps: OS Landranger 180,
Pathfinder SS 41/51.

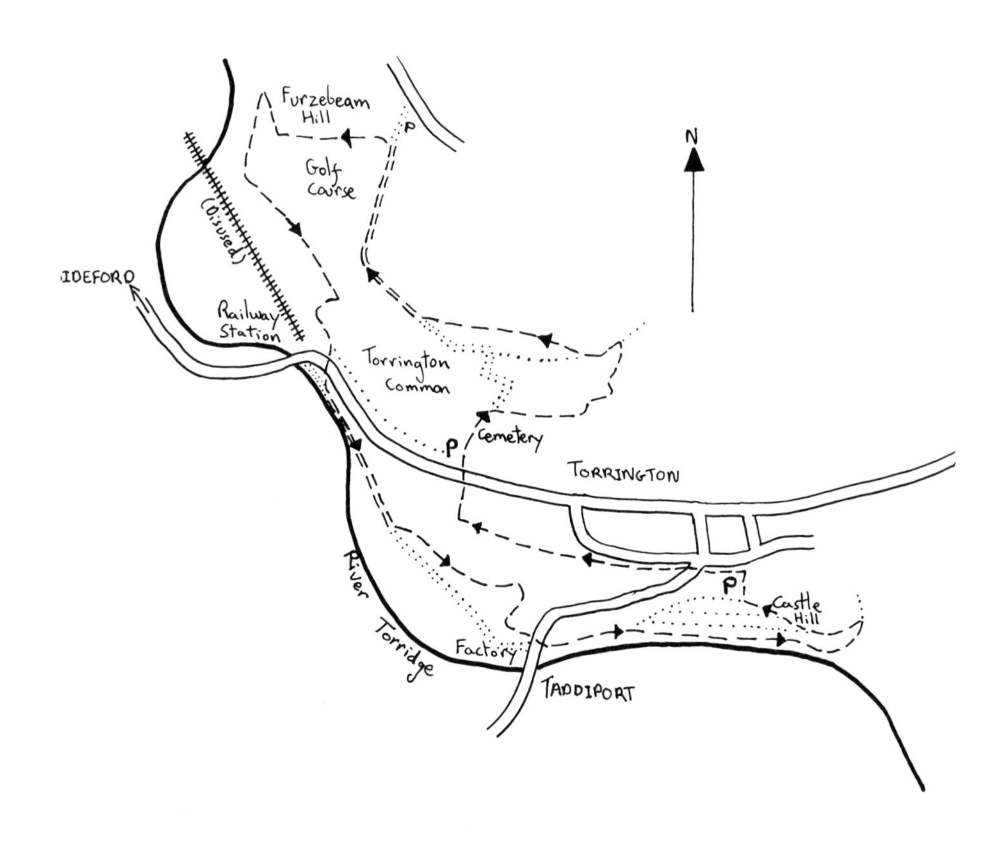

Cross the bridge and turn right following the stream.

On ascending to the higher level path, turn left for a short distance, and right up the steps to a path that follows the boundary of the common at the highest level, with good all round views.

Turn right on the main track (from the car park) and follow it almost to its junction with the road, but aim instead for the golf club house and far boundary hedge.

The golf course started as a simple nine hole course with a wooden shed, but as its popularity increased, so did the standard of the course – and the club house.

Turn left along the hedge – this is to keep you out of the way of golf balls – and at the far end of the course is Furzebeam Hill. From here several church towers can be seen, much of the Torridge valley with part of Weare Giffard, and Beam House below. There used to be two wooden seats here from which to admire the view, but vandals have been at work – why do they never see the need for a seat?

There is much of interest in the valley below; the course of the former railway is obvious, terminating at Torrington railway station, now a public house dominated by a huge storage shed. It is planned that this (the track that is) will become part of the new Tarka Trail footpath, leading eventually to Petersmarland clay works. Less obvious is the old canal, built in 1823 to carry goods from below Bideford to Torrington. The canal terminated at Town Mills, now the Orford Lodge Hotel, situated close to Rosemoor. Much of its course was taken over by the railway that superceded the canal in 1870, but traces of it can still be found, particularly at the foot of Furzebeam Hill where it wound around, following the river bank. The shallow ditch and towpath are quite obvious.

Beam House is now a school but was originally built by the Rolle family, who also built the canal and owned vast areas of land around Torrington. The estates passed to the Clinton family of South Devon in the late 1800's and much of the land was sold. Beam House is older than it looks. From Furzebeam Hill the weir across the Torridge, once popular with salmon fishermen, can be seen and sharp eyes will pick out the small gazebo built in the angle of the garden wall overlooking the river.

Go down through the woods that clothe the steep banks falling to the river, and continue downhill to the field between the river and the railway.

Turn left along the edge of the field and pass the back of Station Cottages, to come out once more by the stream.

Follow the path across the bridge and up the far bank. Here either turn left uphill back to the car park, or for a longer walk, cross over the main road to the footpath opposite.

Look to the right and you will see the small arch in the bridge through which the canal passed.

After only a few yards, take the narrow path to the right that descends via a flight of brick steps alongside the railway viaduct to the former canal path, now used as a road to the creamery factory.

The railway viaduct carried the single track line from Torrington to the clay works at Petersmarland. It was originally only a three foot gauge and was carried on a timber structure. This was replaced by the present viaduct when the line became part of the North Devon & Cornwall Junction Light Railway and was extended to Halwill Junction and thus the rest of the main line network, in 1925.

Turn left along the road; this is the best preserved section of the canal, which was only a few feet deep.

Turn left uphill opposite the entrance to the sewage works, and follow the track to the road, which leads back up to the car park.

Turn right down to the former tollhouse at the end of Taddiport Bridge.

The Torridge Vale Butter Factory, an early farmer's co-operative opened in 1874 utilizing the canal stores. These can still be seen on the left before the inn – but the milk factory outgrew them long ago!

Take the track that leads under Castle Hill, following the line of the old canal. This can be followed almost to its limit, where it meets the main road coming down from Torrington, or the tarmacced path to the left can be taken climbing to the top of Castle Hill.

The commanding position overlooking the river Torridge made it a natural site for a defensive structure, although there are no records of any attacks made upon the town prior to the Civil War. The original castle was built some years prior to 1228, in which year it was ordered to be demolished as it had been built without licence. A somewhat short-lived castle! The walls that now surmount Castle Hill may well be built of the original stone, but at least five centuries later.

Return to the car via the large Castle Hill car park. Turn left at its road entrance (there is a cafe almost opposite).

Follow the lefthand pavement and cross over at the top of Mill Street as it begins its sharp descent. Beyond the Wesleyan chapel is an iron kissing gate leading to a footpath. This joins a quiet road for a short distance before another footpath continues round the hilltop to come out opposite the start point.

Brownsham and Windbury Head

Distance: At least 2 miles.
Maps: OS Landranger 190,
Pathfinder SS 22/32.
NT Leaflet "Clovelly to Hartland Point".

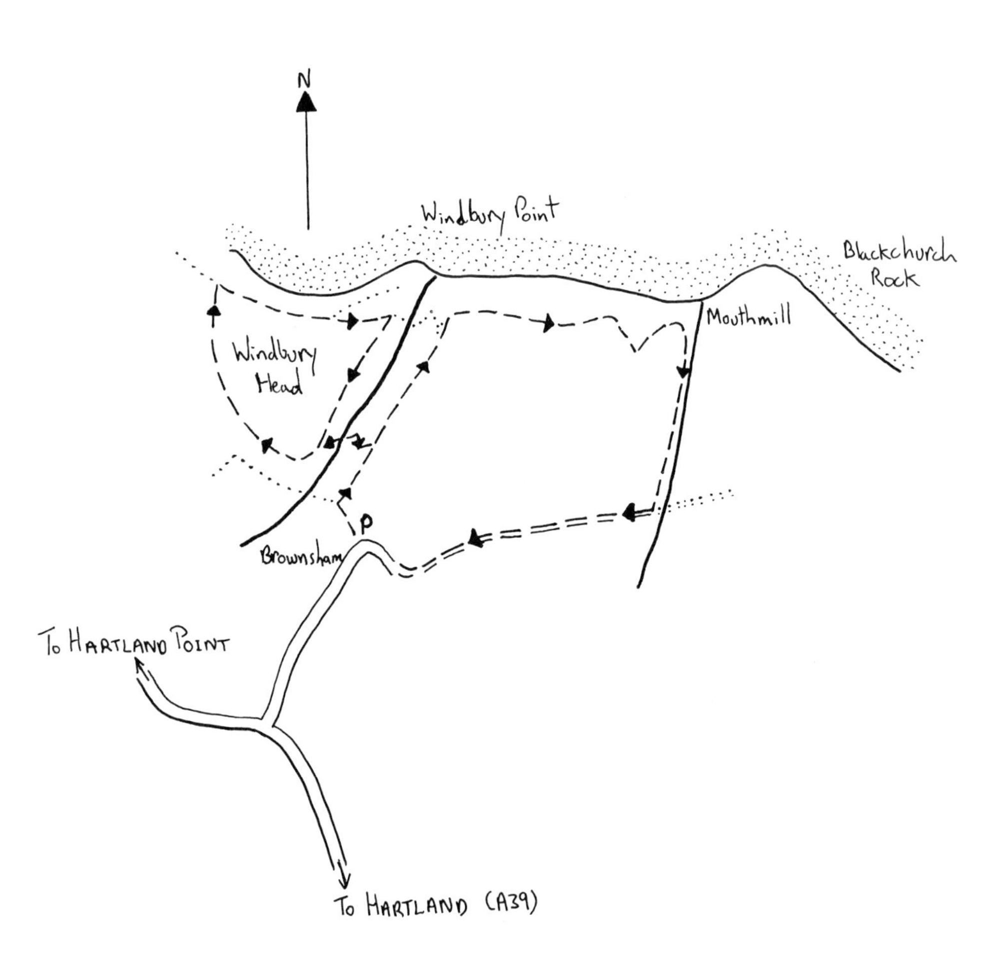

Between Clovelly and Hartland Point lies a somewhat inaccessible area, by-passed by most tourists as it offers nothing at all except beautiful scenery and good walking. Most of it is now owned by the National Trust who provide a car park at **Brownsham**. Closeby are several interesting cottages, also in their ownership but not open to the public. One of them contains an ornamental plaster ceiling of Tudor date which is occasionally on view.

Windbury Head is the site of an iron age camp, which will interest seekers after antiquity. It is also a delectable headland of light woodland, grassy plateaus and sheltered clearings. The views in all directions are magnificent, and it is quite possible to spend a warm day doing nothing very much at all but pottering around Windbury. Springtime sees it at its best, with the fresh young foliage of the beech trees providing a canopy for the carpet of bluebells and primroses. There is wildlife in plenty, including wild bees, as I know to my cost!

From Brownsham, there is the option of walking in either direction, breaking the walk into two, or tackling only one section. For a longer walk, the Clovelly Woodlands can be included (see next chapter).

Directions

The footpath is signposted from the car park. Keep to the hedge and enter the woods through the gate. Follow the path down the valley, and across the stream to meet the coastal footpath.

Turn left on the path which winds inland around Windbury (signposted) then climbs to rejoin the coastal footpath at the cliff edge.

Turn right over the top of Windbury.

It is easy to see why this was chosen as the site of an ancient fort. Little evidence of this remains, but the position still commands wide views over the coast and surrounding countryside. No need to hurry away, and the views on the descent are also good.

Follow the coastpath down, but beware the steep scramble that has been formed down the cliff edge. This leads to the valley bottom where the stream cascades on to the beach, but as neither can be seen and the path is dangerous, it is a pointless deviation.

A new path has been cut ascending the opposite hillside. This is reached by turning left (signposted coastal footpath) and crossing the stream on a new bridge. But easier gradients by far are offered by turning right inland (signposted Brownsham) then down to the first bridge and up the steps to meet the path from Brownsham to Mouthmill.

Brownsham is regained by turning right at this point.

Follow the path to the left across a couple of fields before plunging down through woodland to the beach and 'harbour' of Mouthmill.

From the beach the strange cliff strata can be viewed, and after rain the Windbury waterfall is impressive. At other times it is barely noticeable. Lundy across the Channel is very clear on a good day, and Blackchurch rock to the right of the beach is a continuation of the contorted strata, now worn by the sea to form an arch, with deep rock pools to be explored. Behind it is an almost sheer rock face.

The limekiln is in good repair and would have been used to prepare lime for the estate, offloaded on the beach before burning and then transported, inland, probably by donkey. The kiln was last fired in 1911. Little remains of the estate corn mill except the house. Such is progress that where not so very long ago there was a small, bustling community, all is now deserted except for a few weeks each summer.

To return to Brownsham, take the path inland following the stream. This can be very wet, but it shortly joins the bridle path, now a broad forestry track. Turn right uphill.

Part of the woodlands here are managed as a nature reserve by the Devon Trust and a "tree library" has been planted to include all known native species. Much of the former woodlands are now managed forestry with the inevitable spread of conifers, but the cliff areas remain broadleaved woodland of great beauty.

The track continues uphill and through the farmyard to the car park.

Clovelly Woodlands

The Hobby Drive between Bucks Cross and Clovelly is a popular attraction, and undeniably makes a pleasant walk, especially in springtime when the fresh green of the young beech leaves contrasts with the carpet of bluebells. But the drive is open to cars, and the route is easily followed and requires no description.

Far less frequented and relatively unknown are the woods to the west of Clovelly. Until the creation of the South West Way footpath, visitors were few and far between. The whole area was laid out by Sir James and Lady Diana Hamlyn in the early 1800's, at the same period as the Hobby Drive itself. Although many of the carriage drives are now overgrown, the principal route to Mouthmill is well maintained, and the cliff walk leads past a number of delights discovered by short deviations, such as the little summerhouse amidst the rhododendrons.

Until very recently there were few signposts and fewer restrictions so that a walker could wander at will over the woodlands. But the increasing number of visitors has led to the introduction of small 'private' notices on some of the tracks compensated for by clear marking of those on which one is permitted to walk. The initial notice on the Yellery Gate at the Clovelly end has sadly disappeared.

> *"No right of way, but permission given to use cliff paths to Angels' Wings, Gallantry Bower and Mouth Mill. Please shut the gates,"* it read.

Start Point

Park either in the official Clovelly car park, or for a slightly shorter walk, at the entrance to Clovelly Court and the church where there is limited parking available for visitors to the church. Consciences are salved by doing just this and placing a small donation in the church box. It is a notable church with some interesting memorials both inside and out in the churchyard.

Directions

From the **official car park** walk back down to the road, **not** through the visitor centre, then right along the public road but proceed with care for this is used by the locals, the bus and delivery drivers, and the landrover.

At the road junction turn left and go through the gate (known as the Yellery gate) into the field, following the track around its perimeter. This is now the coast path and is well marked.

From the **church**, follow the drive down to the church and the estate office. This is planted with spring bulbs, flowering cherries and rhododendrons, and is the main drive to Clovelly Court, traditional home of the squires of Clovelly.

Turn left at the estate office, signposted to Court Farm. Take the footpath to the right before reaching the farm, which has recently been designated officially by the Estate, and connects with the coastal footpath (from Yellery Gate).

Turn left when this is reached and follow the yellow arrows which keep close to the cliff edge, avoiding the estate tracks.

Distance: At least 3 miles.
Maps: OS Landranger 190,
Pathfinder SS 22/32.

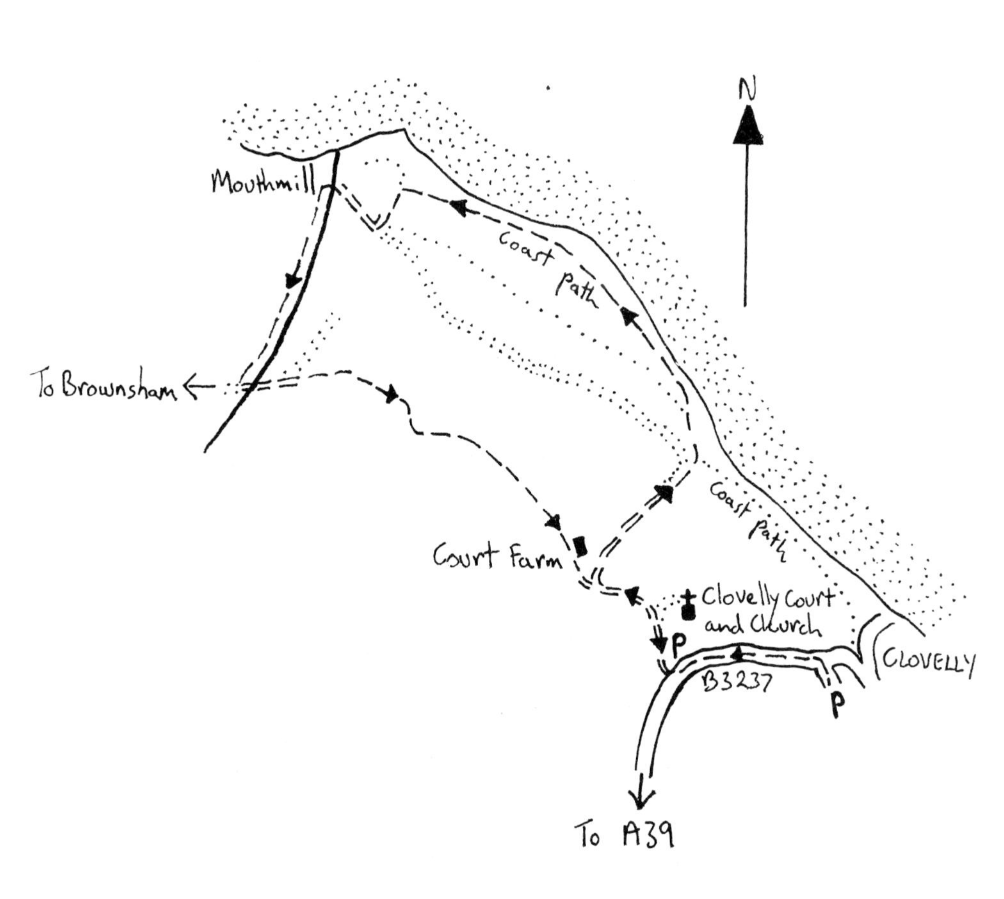

The recently restored Angels' Wings seat is alongside the path and was built so that Sir James Hamlyn could look across Bideford Bay to Youlstone Park the home of his daughter. It is a most unusual and beautiful structure with the shapely roof of cedar shingles supported by four ornately carved wings. Inevitably folk seem incapable of leaving well alone and have carved their own initials in the woodwork.

The waymarked path descends to meet an estate track, and thence to Mouthmill. Formerly the path continued along the cliffs to Gallantry Bower.

This is the quaint name given to the soaring cliffs, here around 400 feet with a sudden drop down to the beach below. Beyond the open headland, and back in the woods once more, look for the cleft in the rocks that leads out on to a ledge perched high up the cliff. This is, or was, Miss Woodall's seat, in memory of a lady who lived at Mouthmill for many years and who loved to sit here watching the gulls wheeling and swooping below. The seat has disappeared, which is a shame as it made a comfortable resting place in this unusual eyrie.

A little further on and looking inland over the woodland is another summerhouse. This substantial building with a fireplace and verandah was built in 1820 and restored in 1935 as an 80th birthday present for Christine Hamlyn, then lady of the manor, whose initials are to be found on so many of the Clovelly cottages. A more modern intrusion is the concrete base of a lookout post above the Blackchurch Rock.

A narrow, twisty path descends to Mouthmill, but it is very steep and involves some ducking and stooping under the stunted oaks, so that it is easier to retrace one's steps to join the estate track.

Down at Mouthmill are the remains of a massive limekiln and cottage, and the old mill itself. Boats used to land on the steep, pebbly beach to unload lime, coal and agricultural and building materials – no easy task. The purpose of the massive retaining wall is not clear. Perhaps it was proposed to build on the level grassy plateau thus created, but this never materialised. It does make an ideal picnic place!

The beach is not good for swimming, being entirely composed of pebbles, and steeply shelving at high tide. There are some large rock pools around Blackchurch rock, and on a calm day swimmers should have no problems.

To return to Clovelly, follow the narrow path inland alongside the stream. This connects with the bridlepath between Clovelly and Brownsham. Here turn left and then right, not on the obvious track, marked 'private' but on the narrow sunken path that climbs steeply up through the woods.

This rocky sunken track is far older than any of the other paths in the woods. Formed through centuries of long usage when the only transport was by packhorse or donkey, the surface has been entirely eroded and is very rough.

It emerges in a field and follows the edge of the woodland to the next hedge, where turn right and walk around the field to join the farm track that leads through the courtyard of Court Farm back to Clovelly church and the road.

The Hartland Cliffs

Magnificent windswept cliffs – sheltered Devon lanes; seabirds wheeling and crying – banks of wild primroses and bluebells; the peacock's unearthly shriek, and stately parkland; North Devon's most impressive church, a small museum and historic quay – even a lighthouse with the relics of the coast's most recent shipwreck – this walk has them all.

The coastal scenery is at its best with the soaring, contorted cliffs and jagged rocks below. Aptly described as "some seven miles of the wildest and grandest cliff scenery to be met with in the whole of Devon," the cliffs of Hartland are rewarding and exhilarating. Tough and exposed, facing all that the Atlantic has to throw at them, there are times when it is all but impossible to stand against the winds, and on such days not many venture onto the headlands.

There are no houses, no roads, few trees and very limited access to the shoreline. Sandy beaches and clifftop parking belong to the Bristol Channel coast, and further down in Cornwall. Banks of pebbles lie at the foot of the cliffs, and at low tide flat ribs of rocks are exposed, with varying degrees of sand. Some years there is plenty, turning many of the small bays into beaches; other years there is none at all and swimmers have to make do with the rocks.

But there is a grandeur about these cliffs, a satisfaction to be gained from striding out mile after mile in the bracing air that lives long in the memory when other, more tame walks are forgotten.

Between Hartland Point and Hartland Quay is an area of great geological interest, as well as the more apparent rugged beauty. The Point itself forms virtually a right angle between the Bristol Channel coast and the Atlantic. Here the cliffs are over 300 feet in height. The streams that drain in swift, steep courses to the sea excite expert interest with talk of canyons, anticlines, undercuts, gutter falls and sea-dissected valleys.

Distance: Full distance around 5 miles.
Maps: OS Landranger 190,
Pathfinder SS 22/32
"Westward Ho! to Welcombe" by the author.

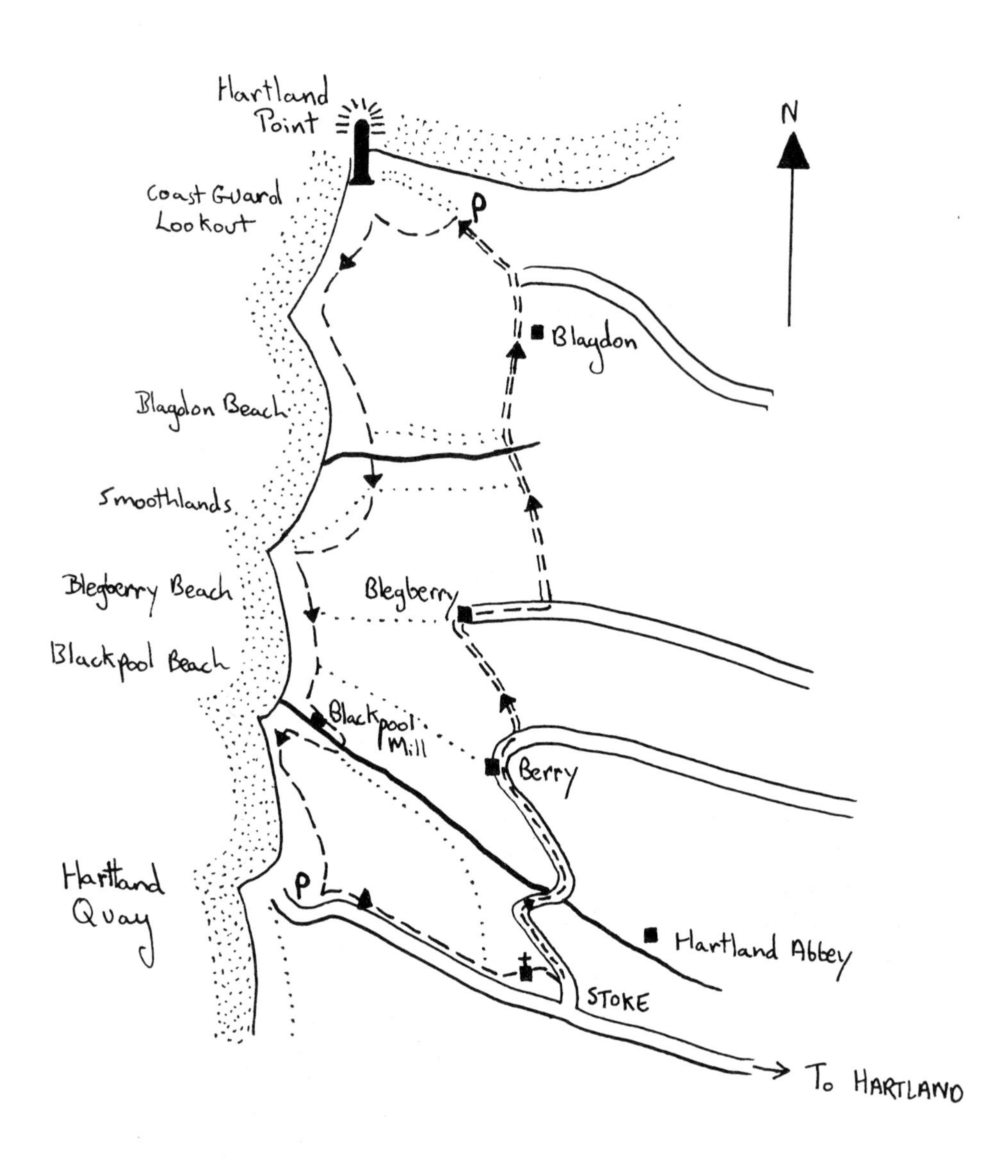

Inland, for those who like a contrast and who hate retracing their steps however good the views, is a series of sunken forgotten lanes, now largely impassable to wheeled vehicles. These connect Hartland Quay with Hartland Point, making an easier, quicker alternative to the coast path.

Although the walk is grand taken in either direction, I have a distinct preference for following the lanes from south to north (Quay to Point) and the coast in reverse (Point to Quay). Not only are the gradients much easier in this direction, but the views are also finer. If the coast path is followed from south to north, the view terminates at the Cow and Calf rocks just before Hartland Point, whatever the visibility, whilst on a clear day walkers facing south will have the whole panorama of the Cornish cliffs as far as Trevose Head in front of them. It is here on the cliffs that one will wish to linger, and there are many suitable spots. As you are now returning homewards the time element is not so important – I take around one hour to reach the Point and anything from 1½ hours to four or more to return!

The walk has the further advantage that it is possible to work out figures of eight, or decide the coast is preferable and abandon the lanes, or run for shelter if the coast becomes unfriendly, or shorten the walk to suit. The range is endless and the choice is yours.

Start Point

There are two possible starting points. Both Hartland Point and Hartland Quay have large car parks, grassy areas and good seaviews, and for which there is a modest charge in the season. At the Point a refreshment hut offers teas, coffees, snacks and homemade cakes etc. in the season. At Hartland Quay the hotel is open all the year round with excellent homemade food in the bar, and cream teas in season. There is also a gift shop and museum. The disadvantage is that to reach this mecca of civilisation involves a steep descent to the cliff base – followed by the inevitable climb back. The trick is to leave the car at the top car park, moving it down on one's return. If you are starting from the Point, then you have been warned!

Directions

From **Hartland Quay**

Follow the footpath inside the hedge boundary with the road. Begin at the gate beyond the former Rocket House, and continue along the "secret" path between the houses and the hedge hidden from the road, to the church.

The row of cottages were built for the coastguards, and the small stone building beyond them was used as a mortuary for the drowned sailors washed up from time to time.

Cross the slate stile into the churchyard and follow the path to a similar stile at the far end.

A visit to the church of St Nectan is recommended. North Devon's cathedral is a lovely building, full of light and majesty with a tower of just under 130 feet, the tallest in the county. It entirely dominates the small hamlet of Stoke, but it was built originally to serve the needs of the Abbey in the valley below, rather than the people of Hartland.

Turn left down the narrow lane beneath a high canopy of trees and descend to the Abbey River, crossed on an ancient two arch stone bridge.

Across the parkland is Hartland Abbey, home of the Stucley family. The original Abbey was dissolved in 1539 and almost all traces of it have disappeared. The estate was a gift from Henry VIII to the keeper of his wine cellar, from whom the present owners descend. The property has never been sold.

In front of the gothic front of the Abbey are several fine trees; sadly a most venerable oak was blown over in the gales of 1990.

The pond is believed to be the medieval abbey fish pond.

The Abbey is open to the public on Wednesdays and Sundays during the summer. The most unnatural sound of a peacock screaming can be disconcerting if one doesn't know the cause.

Continue on the lane uphill to Berry Farm.

Here a 'new wing' was added to a far older farmhouse. Berry may have gained its imposing facade when owned by a relative of the Luttrells at the Abbey. It is a most interesting building – notice the pigeon holes in the farmhouse wall, still regularly occupied, and the different levels of the roofs.

Pass between the house and the buildings, keeping to the road, and continue to the cross roads – or fourcross way in local language.

Cross over and take the 'green lane' down into the next valley. This old lane, with overgrown hedgerows, climbs uphill to the remarkable farm of Blegberry. The footpath turns to the right by the cottages but this means missing the fortified and ancient farmhouse, with its splendid range of farmbuildings, worth more than a second glance. Follow the track around the walls and farmhouse.

Blegberry was possibly an early hill fort. The farmhouse was built in 1627 and was fortified during the Civil War when the owner was a Royalist supporter and an unpopular tax collector. Was the new front built to keep up with the neighbours at Berry?

The extensive stone-built farm buildings with mounting steps, lofts and stables give way to their modern counterparts. It is difficult not to make unfavourable comparisons between the stone and slate and concrete and corrugated, and hope that it is the former that will survive.

Follow the metalled road inland until a lane turns down to the left (signposted). Follow this to the next valley.

From here the coastguard lookout of Hartland Point and the cliffs above Shipload Bay are visible. The valley of Titchberry Water, crossed by a new wooden bridge, is a delight in springtime with daffodils and primroses. (A short cut can be taken by using the footpath that commenced before the footbridge is reached. This contours along the valley side to meet the coast path.)

The path follows the stream for a short distance before joining the track down from Blagdon Farm.

For Hartland Point, turn right and follow the track through the farmyard and over the top to the Point car park. The track to the left leads down to Blagdon beach.

From **Hartland Point**

Leave the car park by the road to the lighthouse and take the coast path that climbs up some steps just beyond the wall on the left. This leads to the coastal lookout.

From the lookout the views are extensive. The top of St Nectan's church tower rises above the fields and the arched folly above the quay is prominent. Beyond, the cliffs of Cornwall stretch away.

Until very recently the lookout was a welcome sight to all sailors who had spent long days crossing the Atlantic, being the first inhabited building. It was also welcome to the many local craft who have to negotiate the tricky waters of the Hartland Point race. Now it is abandoned, a victim of some strange policy that insists the safety of the seas is best maintained by men sitting in offices and rooms far inland and out of sight and sound of salt water. Sadly a fatality occurred in 1989 in the waters off Hartland Point when a local fisherman got into difficulties and his companion was drowned. Below the lookout is the Lighthouse and that, too, is now unmanned. A shipwrecked mariner would search here for help in vain, and it was as recent as 1983 that the 'Johanna' ran aground under the cliffs, on New Year's Eve, fortunately with no loss of life. Below the lookout is all that remains of her, a striking reminder, if any is needed, of the vital importance of all such coastal lookouts.

The Lighthouse was first lit in 1874. It was built on a particularly difficult site that had to be surveyed from the sea, with the access road blasted from the cliffs before building could commence. A supporting platform was constructed more recently because of problems from continuing rock falls.

All these cliffs are dangerous and should be treated with respect from both above and below.

Follow the coastal path which is clearly defined.

Look across the valley to the unusual formation opposite. This is Smoothlands, and is a sea-dissected valley – a very good example apparently. Originally the stream that now reaches the sea at Blagdon flowed through this valley (now dry-ish) to reach the sea at its far end. At some stage the sea eroded the cliffs sufficiently far inland to cut the river and alter its course.

The two huge logs are all that is left of a large 'stick' of mahogany, part of a cargo lost in Bideford Bay some years ago. Obviously it was 'salvaged' and then left here, too heavy to shift further. Now beetle infestation has made serious inroads and it will be interesting to see how long the mahogany lasts. There is a beach here of sorts, reached by a narrow difficult path.

The path leaves Blagdon by a wooden bridge close to the caravan, and climbs the cliff. The coastal footpath descends to Smoothlands, and reascends at the far end. This is unnecessary as a footpath continues around the field above the valley and the two meet up when the coast is regained. Here there is a well placed bench, for the views down the coast are worth stopping to appreciate, with the cluster of white buildings of Hartland Quay in view for the first time.

The next valley is Blegberry, where another small river tumbles over the cliff edge. It is crossed by an ancient stone bridge, evidence perhaps of a former coastguard lookout path along these cliffs. Traces of an old path do survive, but the influx of modern boots with the creation of the South West Way has obliterated much. It has also made walking easier with the provision of footbridges and stiles – but removed a great deal of the challenge that previously existed when crossing streams was not always easy, and the path neither marked nor clearly defined. Those were the days!

The "beach" at Blegberry is surprisingly popular. The path down is very awkward, and the ugly metal handrail is essential. This path is in danger of collapse (such falls usually only happen during the winter months) so that a new path may be formed in future years. In a good year there is a respectable sandy beach between the rock beds. In other years there is none at all and children splash happily in the rockpools.

The path climbs up, past an incongruous modern house, to the next height. The track inland leads to Berry Farm.

Blackpool Valley is a particular delight. Through it flows the Abbey river, longest of the Hartland streams. Here was the Abbey mill, now a picturesque cottage, dating from at least the sixteenth century but working up until around 1820.

The Abbey River is noted as a good example of a mature canyon and the evolution of a waterfall. Considerable changes have been recorded in the formation of the falls since the beginning of the century, and old photographs show a distinct fall of around twenty feet.

Access to the beach here is easy, but it is all pebbles and rocks, and rarely any use for swimming. The river can only be crossed when the water is low.

The official path goes inland past the mill and right through a metal kissing gate to cross on the substantial old stone bridge.

The path to the left leads up to Stoke and the church, through delightful bluebell woods.

To reach Hartland Quay bear right back to the cliffs and up the last incline to what used to be known as Warren cliff.

This name historically denoted an area where rabbits were positively encouraged, providing a valuable source of food, in this case for the inhabitants of the Abbey.

The stone arch building is generally thought to have been built as a focal point, or folly, by the owners of the Abbey, and is believed to date from around 1730 but its acutal purpose, if any, seems obscure unless it was as a lookout.

Hartland Quay and refreshments lie down the roadway.

There was once a quay – a long, snaking stone structure dating from at least the early 17th century. It was kept in good repair until 1887 when it was breached, and by 1893 the last cargo was landed. The little port, surely one of the most exposed and romantic anywhere around our coasts, supported a thriving community of limeburners, mariners, fishermen, a malthouse and pub, a bank printing its own money, and a coastguard's cottage. The former cottages and storehouses are today the Quay hotel, and the museum which houses a fascinating display of the history of the quay and of the shipwrecks once so much a part of life on the North Devon coast.

In recent years it has been the turn of the hotel buildings to suffer and a former shed that bordered the car park has disappeared. This area is now unsafe. The cliffs are altering all the time and although there are unlikely to be dramatic changes in our lifetime, continual falls necessitate alterations to the coast path in places and at all times care is needed.

The beach at Hartland Quay is usually a good place for a swim. A recent fisherman's jetty has been constructed which makes a good diving platform.

Tail Piece

It is interesting that something as simple and instinctive as putting one foot in front of the other can be the means of opening up a whole new world to many of us. To some it is still a form of torture to be avoided at all costs; feet were made to operate car pedals, not walk. Leaving such folk where they belong – in the car parks – there are vast areas waiting to be discovered and explored. And the only expense is a sensible pair of shoes and a map. Not even the latter is essential as many of the routes within the National Park are so well signposted it would be difficult to go astray. Walkers with a little more curiosity and spirit of adventure will benefit from a map and a guidebook or two. There is much to be seen that will otherwise be missed, and reading maps is the bad weather consolation of all true walkers. They bring back memories of splendid walks already completed, and inspire one to plan routes for the better weather to come.

Time was when no-one actually went walking for sheer enjoyment. The lower classes had no time and the gentry went on horseback. The possible exceptions were a few country parsons and a few discerning energetic eccentrics. Walking, as such, was considered unsuitable for ladies. Their complexions and constitutions were surely too delicate; sunburn was so unbecoming, and they might muddy their gowns. Walking was the means of getting from one point to another employed by those who had no means of transport other than their own two legs.

The network of footpaths that exists today is largely a legacy left by villagers travelling between home and village or place of employment, or to church. They did not set out to scale the highest point, far from it, nor to take in the local beauty spot. Such paths are of modern origins. Old paths and pony routes are usually recognizable by the very fact that they take the easiest and most sheltered route, wend their way around a hill rather than go straight up, and in many instances keep to the shelter of a hedge or ancient wall. Generations of packhorses and villagers have even worn the deeply sunken lanes, protected by high hedgebanks and overhanging trees. We who walk these routes today are following the footsteps of those countless men and women who patiently toiled and gave only fleeting glances to the beauty around them. We do well to remember them, and take nothing for granted in our more leisured age that gives us the time to walk, quite simply, for pleasure.